Contents

Preface

I have divided this volume into three parts. The first chapter is an introduction to the history and the form of Gothic fiction, and it is also an outline of some contemporary criticism of the form. Due to a lack of space I have confined myself to a highly selective grouping of Gothic texts (novels rather than poetry or drama) which I feel gives a representative flavour of the Gothic mode from the late eighteenth to the early nineteenth century (form Ann Radcliffe to Mary Shelley). In the second chapter I give my own reading of **Dracula** which comes out of a broadly Foucauldian perspective. I explain in this chapter what such a perspective implies and I will develop an historical reading of the novel which embraces particular aspects of the fin-de-siècle. The third chapter is an outline of various critical readings of Stoker's novel. These three chapters hang loosely together and they can be read as separate entities. I have devised the volume in this way so that the reader can dip into it as required. The bibliography provides an indication of where other readings can be found.

This volume was conceived because of student demand on a course of Gothic fiction at Sheffield Hallam University. This volume can only give a cursory insight into **Dracula** but I hope that it will prove to be a helpful introduction to some of the issues which surround the novel.

Chapter One - The Gothic

In this chapter I examine a variety of early Gothic
texts. My reasons for making this selection are
because they will give a feel of the rhythms of the
Gothic over a particular period as well as
establishing its themes and formal features. This
account of these texts is not intended to be
exhaustive and the bibliography indicates where
more indepth analysis can be found. After
exploring some Gothic texts I then briefly outline
some of the registers which are employed by
critics of the Gothic. In this chapter I look at a
grouping of Gothic writing which shows how
writers respond to each other. My argument is that
Matthew Lewis responds to the early work of Ann
Radcliffe and that Radcliffe subsequently makes
her own response to Lewis. I then discuss
Frankenstein in order to show how the Gothic
moves away from the concerns of the early writers
to embrace the complexities of Romanticism. This
reading of these novels is a brief outline but I feel
that it gives some idea of the changes in the form

Introduction

during its early period. When discussing Radcliffe and Lewis I initially give a brief plot synopsis of the novels because these may not be familiar to readers, and the very complexity of these plots are used in order to create a Gothic ambience of suspense and are thus integral to its form. Two registers which I refer to here are that of Sensibility and that of the Sublime. To some degree I assume some prior knowledge of these terms in the reader, but what I mean by these terms is that sensibility can be defined as an emotional faculty possessed by the hero/heroine which marks out their virtue. This emotional receptivity means that a character is emotionally sophisticated enough to respond to the higher realm of virtue which is to be found in the sublime. The 'evil' characters in these novels possess no such sensibility and are so cut off from a world of integrity and virtue. The sublime is that experience, fashionable in the eighteenth century and central to Romanticism, which suggests the existence of a higher realm which frequently, although not unproblematically, implies the existence of God through nature. To be unreceptive to this noumenal (non-phenomenal) world means to be estranged from God, a defining characteristic of the early Gothic villain.

The Gothic - Ann Radcliffe

One of the striking features of the Gothic is the credence which it gives to irrational moments. It is a form which posits the existence of various impossibilities such as ghosts, vampires, ghouls, and demons amongst many other fantastical forms. The Gothic landscape is littered with ruins, beset by inhospitable nature and peopled with malign aristocrats. This is of course a clichéd picture of the form, but it is true to say that the Gothic does rely upon a repertoire of stock props. What is important to consider is the way that individual texts reconfigure these props. Reading the Gothic is more than an exercise in convention spotting, rather we have to consider what significance is attached to these conventions by particular writers. A castle in one text, for example, might symbolise institutional authority, in another it might have an overtly phallic patriarchal significance (although the one reading does not necessarily exclude the other). To this end different writers draw upon an existing pool of devices in order to inflect them in often unique ways. The Gothic is therefore more elastic than a purely structural account might suggest. I will begin by discussing the work of Ann Radcliffe because it is in her work that many of the Gothic props found in earlier, cruder, novels are given new and interesting reworkings. Firstly I want to locate Radcliffe in her historical context because this helps to illuminate why it is that she writes in a certain way, in order to do this it is necessary to explore the philosophical context of her writing.

Radcliffe's Gothic is influenced by Edmund Burke's important treatise **A Philosophical Enquiry into the Origins of Our Ideas of the Beautiful and the Sublime** (1757) (1). The sublime is an important register in the later half of the eighteenth century and the beginning of the nineteenth century. It defines a state in which the subject feels an overwhelming affinity with some aspect of nature, and as such it seems to be a positive force because it offers the subject a glimpse of a greater world (noumenal rather than phenomenal), however, it is also a negative force because such is the power of the emotion that it annihilates (on a mental level) the subject. In his treatise Burke suggests that the true source of the sublime is a feeling of Terror. It is how we respond to this terror which (in a move later more clearly spelt out by Kant (2)) defines our moral integrity. The importance of this is that Burke was formulating an idea of what it meant to be a subject, of what is meant by subjectivity. It is, significantly, an exploration of a subjectivity which is situated in a potentially malevolent setting. What Burke states is that there exists a psychology of fear, and it was this idea of a dark psychology which was absorbed by the Gothic both as an aesthetic (creating narrative suspense) and as a psychology of the Gothic character.

The importance of Radcliffe to the Gothic is that she introduced the concept of sensibility into the Gothic novel. This notion implies that the heroine's possession of it means that she is protected from malevolent forces. When looking at her work it is important to observe how she combines ideas of sensibility, class, latent sexuality, and 'evil' in her work; issues which resurface in **Dracula**.

The Mysteries of Udolpho (1794)(3) tells the story of the perils confronted by the heroine, Emily St Aubert, who when she is orphaned is taken into the care of her Aunt and her Aunt's new husband, Montoni. Montoni keeps Emily and her Aunt virtual prisoners in the Castle of Udolpho. Montoni's aim is to gain access to Emily's family money so that he can maintain his dissipated life style. Emily's Aunt is murdered but Emily escapes this danger and is able to renew her life with her paramour, Valencourt, who has fallen into a dissipated lifestyle of his own (although one from which he can be redeemed). Whilst at Udolpho Emily is confronted by a series of apparently supernatural circumstances which she later feels might have been either the product of her overactive imagination, or else tricks played upon her by the evil Montoni; 'I have heard almost all of them explained.'(p.491). However, Emily's fears are no less real for all of that. What Emily discovers at Udolpho is a demonic form of patriarchal power. The story is concerned with exposing the authority of a character like Montoni who is closely associated with female incarceration. To this degree the novel possesses a subtle form of feminism because Emily triumphs over Montoni and over her fears. The novel therefore fulfils Ellen Moers (4) identification of the female Gothic as a type of writing which is characterised by social optimism. Emily is subject to Burkean Terrors but she is able to overcome them (in a non-Burkean move) by supplanting them with an idea of the natural sublime. It is this idea of the sublime, a heightened emotional state

Udolpho

7

which suggests the oneness between nature and its creator, which is the true salvation for Emily. It is the sublime which is consistently contrasted with the synthetic status of Art and the cultural function of language. Radcliffe writes of the Alps that, 'And here such scenes of sublimity opened upon them as no colours of language must dare to paint!'(p.163), which suggests that there exists a compulsive moral imperative behind all of this; an imperative which a character such as Emily is susceptible to because she possesses the necessary sensibility. It is this sensibility which also suggests her vulnerability when Terror takes on its Burkean guise. This is apparent during her discovery of a skull behind a veil at Udolpho, Emily's terror is described in terms of:-

> [...]a Terror of this nature, as it occupies and expands the mind, and elevates it to high expectation, is purely sublime, and leads us, by a kind of fascination, to seek even the object, from which we appear to shrink. (p.248).

Terror becomes psychologised here in ways which echo its Burkean form, however, she introduces an idea of the natural sublime (elsewhere) which is superior in power to the Terror of Burke's sublime. As suggested, Radcliffe achieves this by setting up an opposition between aesthetic practice and natural splendour. The feelings of terror evoked in the above passage are belied by her confrontation with what turns out to be an unreal skull. Likewise, after Emily's visit to an opera we find that, '[...]where Emily was not so charmed but that, when she remembered the scene she had just quitted, she felt how infinitely inferior all the splendour of art is to the sublimity of nature.'(p.189). It is this sensitivity to nature, this sensibility, which marks out her virtue and is the trait that contrasts her with the 'evil' characters in the text. What is latent in Radcliffe's novel is the role of sexuality. During Emily's confinement at Udolpho she is implicitly threatened with the possibility of rape; this is something which Emily, for all her sexual innocence, is only too aware of as a genuine threat. This might therefore point towards a paradox in the novel which is that the virtue inherent in sensibility is somewhat compromised by Emily's possession of a sexually knowing imagination. It is this theme of sexuality which is so important in the Gothic and which is central to a reading of **Dracula** will now outline some of the features of Matthew Lewis' novel **The Monk** (1796)(5) because his writing is to some extent a reply to Radcliffe's coyness over sexuality and he also offers a trenchant repudiation of Radcliffe's faith in a protecting sensibility.

Lewis' **The Monk** (1796) tells the story of a prominent Spanish monk called Ambrosio. Ambrosio is described as approaching a time in his life when he will be subject to sexual urges (the novel suggests that this is because of his age, nearing thirty). Ambrosio is introduced to sexual pleasure by Matilda who is the devil's emissary in disguise. Ambrosio becomes enamoured with one of his parishioners, Antonia, and he kills her mother, Elvira, in order to gain access to Antonia whom he poisons, abducts, rapes, and murders.

Lewis

One revelation is that Ambrosio is the long lost son of Elvira and he has therefore added the crime (sin) of incest to his others. Ambrosio is finally killed by Satan for his soul and he is subjected to a long and painful death. There are various subplots in the novel which suggest that even the virtuous are subject to desire, but these subplots are brought to largely consoling conclusions. The novel's Spanish setting also evidences various degrees of anti-Catholicism as monks and nuns alike are shown to be inherently corrupt.

The basic argument (if it can be so called) in **The Monk** concerns the supposed nature of male heterosexual desire. The novel implies that religion is an unnatural form which represses that desire. Morality is largely a personal matter which contrasts with its institutional manifestation in the church. The 'healthy' subject has to enter into society because the isolation imposed by a monastic life compromises what it means to be fully human. Lorenzo explains in the opening scene of the novel what it is that Ambrosio has to contend with:-

> [...]now, when obliged by the duties of his situation he must enter occasionally into the world and be thrown into the way of temptation, it is now that it behoves him to show the brilliance of his virtue. The trial is dangerous; he is just at that period of life when the passions are most vigorous, unbridled, and despotic. (p.16).

It is a trial which Ambrosio is unequal to, but precisely because it is unfair of society (and religion) to expect him to succeed. It is the unnatural isolation of Ambrosio which ill-prepares him for the world and which makes his decline all the more dramatic. Whereas in the work of Radcliffe definitions of evil are easily discernable in Lewis these definitions are blurred. The question which is constantly posed concerns the nature of evil itself. Is Ambrosio inherently evil? Or does the repressive effects of a monastic life, combined with the devil's influence, excuse Ambrosio's actions? One of the striking features of **The Monk** is the way that it naturalises a version of male sexuality; this sexuality has to find a 'natural' outlet, so the novel implies, otherwise it will come out in a twisted fashion. It is for this reason that it is easy to see why the Gothic has appealed to psychoanalytical types of criticism.

It is with the character of Antonia that Lewis revises the Radcliffean idea about the existence of a protecting sensibility. Ambrosio is ultimately punished for his actions but there exists no corresponding divine providence which protects the virtuous. David Punter writes about Antonio's sensibility that, '[...]Lewis has her abducted, poisoned, raped and murdered as a savage indication of the inadequacy of this faith.'(p.74)(6).

Lewis' novel attacks the notion of sensibility and criticises the church. His novel is also replete with images of mass destruction which suggest an historical inflection by anxieties over the French Revolution. Lewis also implies that sexuality plays a part in all of this, a part which is left at a covert level in the work of Radcliffe.

11

So, **The Monk** appears to be essentially concerned with the dangers associated with repression, a view which contrasts starkly with that of Radcliffe. For Radcliffe repression is important because it is carried out for the greater good; rather than being crippling, repression indicates virtue because it suggests that people can move beyond their self-interests. I will now explore Radcliffe's **The Italian** because it is a response to **The Monk**.

Back to Radcliffe

Radcliffe's **The Italian** (1797)(7) has a traditional form which is familiar from the work of Horace Walpole, this form being that of the found document. It is this document which is given to an English tourist visiting Italy and which helps to establish the novel's anti-Catholicism. The story appears to be that of a simple romance; Ellena, an apparent commoner, is courted by the aristocratic Vivaldi, Vivaldi's mother, the marchesa, finds out and seeks counsel from a father Schedoni about how she can stop these liaisons. Schedoni, about whom there had been rumours that he was an assassin before entering monastic life, advises the Marchesa that it is necessary to have Ellena abducted and ultimately killed. Subsequently Ellena is kept as a virtual prisoner in a nunnery. Vivaldi rescues her and they plan an impromptu wedding which is disturbed by people acting as agents for the Inquisition and Vivaldi is taken into custody. Ellena is handed over to Schedoni who intends to kill her but is unable to do so because, catching sight of a locket which she is wearing, he mistakenly believes himself to be her father. Eventually Vivaldi is released from the Inquisition and Schedoni's testimony, whilst he is dying, explains many of the mysteries which concern his past. Ellena finds that her real mother is alive and discovers that she is of aristocratic birth; consequently the marriage between Vivaldi and Ellena which concludes the novel can take place without class positions being compromised.

This is obviously a highly complicated plot which on a narrative level creates suspense through its narrative twists and slow revelation of secrets. The novel uses various ploys which can be found in **The Monk**, in Radcliffe's novel we find a malevolent monk, the demonisation of some aspects of institutional religion, as well as greater embellishment upon the staging effects to be found in the court of the Inquisition. Ellena is a similar character to Emily sharing with her a protecting sensibility; again there is a providential design which protects the virtuous and punishes the wicked. The novel's avowed anti-Catholicism is more ambiguous than that of Lewis'; although the church and its agents are vilified there is a sense in which Catholicism is maintained at a different level. Schedoni is the wicked monk here, but he is to some degree redeemed through his refusal to kill Ellena, subsequently he makes a death bed confession and receives a form of absolution. One irony in the novel then is that for all its anti-Catholic content it also exonerates Catholicism in the treatment of Schedoni. 'Evil' is defined in this novel as a temporary falling away from virtue, characters such as Schedoni and the Marchesa are only nominally evil because they can be redeemed. 'Evil' is therefore a fragile concept in this novel, and this is in contrast to how it is formulated in a later novel such as **Dracula**. In Stoker's novel the vampire is inherently evil whereas in Radcliffe the idea of evil is more fluid and is linked to her particular construction of the subject.

This becomes apparent when we observe how true and false are defined in the novel. For Radcliffe, truth is associated with an authenticity which is found in sensibility. It is this sensibility which supplies the opportunity for transcendence; after Ellena's aunt has died, for example, Ellena is granted temporary rest on her country journey to the convent and finds that:-

> Here, the objects seem to impart somewhat of their own force, their own sublimity, to the soul. It is scarcely possible to yield to the pressure of misfortune while we walk, as with the Deity, amidst his most stupendous works! (p.63).

The sublime is a consoling pantheistic force and this signals the truth about nature and the truth to be found in the virtuous apprehending subject. It is this idea of a natural truth which contrasts with the early descriptions of Schedoni:-

> [...]he cared not for truth, nor sought it by bold and broad argument, but loved to exert the wily cunning of his nature in hunting it through artificial perplexities. At length, from a habit of intricacy and suspicion, his vitiated mind could receive nothing for truth, which was simple and easily comprehended. (p.34).

Schedoni is therefore debarred from the simple truth of nature and is thus estranged from "the Deity". The possibilities of the sublime are important in this context because it becomes an experience in which, if perhaps only provisionally, social distinctions become erased. Also, it is the place where gender distinctions are held in abeyance (the sublime taking you out of your social self) and the novel replaces the idea of sexual passion with the passion which is stimulated (sublimated) in moments of sublime reverie. I write that the sublime provisionally erases social distinctions because although sensibility appears to be democratic (it is potentially open to everyone) in reality this is not the case. Paulo, Vivaldi's loyal servant, for example, is not moved in the same way as either Vivaldi or Ellena when the three encounter the mountain scenery above the lake of Celano. Vivaldi and Ellena are moved to sublime rapture whereas Paulo's response is not quite so ecstatic, "'what a prospect is here! It reminds me of home; it is almost as pleasant as the bay of Naples!'"(p.158). Such a comparison means that Paulo has missed the point about an omnipresent pantheism. The novel is also concerned with issues such as patriarchy and class. The revelation at the end that Ellena is of noble birth signals a conservative conclusion which maintains the class status quo through her marriage to Vivaldi.

These three novels, **Udolpho, The Monk** and **The Italian**, are an important grouping because we can see how it is that they respond to each other and how it is that the use of similar Gothic props (monks, nuns, the Inquisition) are used to construct contrasting versions of events. There exist other similarities between them which are identified by Punter in the following way:-

> [...]all three of the books are, like so many romantic works, thematically centred on the complex relations between solitude, society and the imagination, between the individual's liberation into the worlds of 'fancy' and his (sic) outward subservience to the bands of convention and repression. Thus they are essentially explorations of the relation between the individual and his environment. (p.73).

In Radcliffe, this concern with the interaction between the individual and the environment is revealed through the way that the landscape prompts particular feelings; with Lewis it is the case that the environment (here a social one) produces repression. What both writers share at heart is the Romantic view that the social environment is in no way foundational in constructing the subject. I will now go on to discuss how Mary Shelley's **Frankenstein** (8) recasts Romantic thought through its sceptical approach towards Romantic abstractions. I want to explore this novel because it is a good example of how the Gothic constructs counter-cultural claims; it also focuses upon issues related to how the outsider is perceived, issues which are also relevant to a reading of **Dracula**.

Mary Shelley

The initially striking feature of Shelley's novel is its convoluted structure, the novel being an account of a conversation between Victor Frankenstein and Robert Walton. Victor takes over control of the narrative at various moments, but at its basic level we have the account told by the monster to Victor which is then told to Walton and which is then passed on by him in the form of a letter to his sister. This means that information is mediated many times over and it highlights one of the novel's central themes which is that of communication. **Dracula** also follows an epistolary format which, in a different way, emphasises that information is constitutive of forensic evidence. In **Frankenstein**, communication is problematised on several levels, one notable factor which causes such a problematisation is the clash which exists between social responsibility and personal desire. Ultimately it seems as though Victor is punished for having created a monster which he refuses to take responsibility for, however, as I will suggest, the picture is more complex than this.

Firstly, the novel is indebted to notions of the subject which are familiar from the philosophical works of Locke and Hartley. The idea that the subject is constituted through a series of psycho-social associations means that Shelley is coming from a different perspective than either Radcliffe or Lewis. The monster is a social product, but significantly, he is perceived as a psychological (and social) threat. Chris Baldick in **Frankenstein: Myth, Monstrosity and**

17

Nineteenth Century Writing (9) points out that the words monster and demonstrate come from the same etymological root 'monstrare' or 'to show' and that there exists a lengthy tradition of writing which regards monstrosity as representing (displaying) moral vices. There is thus a tradition of writing (most of Baldick's examples are from Shakespeare) which establishes simple connections between physical mutilation and moral mutilation. **Frankenstein** shows the injustice which is inherent in this way of seeing. The monster is defined by his speech and not by his looks and he compromises other characters' understanding of nature because he is simultaneously unnatural (a surgically produced subject) and natural (he is made up from natural parts). Shelley therefore critiques the way that a society sees as well as debunking certain elements of Romantic Idealism. It is this latter idealism which is associated with abstract thought by Shelley (as in the type of abstraction found in theories of the sublime) and this is analogously manifested through Victor's science. Victor's scientific practice is a predominantly theoretical one and he fails to think through the ramifications of the practical implementation of this theory. His desertion of the product of this theory points towards Victor's social irresponsibility. Romantic Idealism is more concerned with obviating the social world than with understanding it, and Shelley's project is to expose the poverty of social vision which is inherent to this idealism.

For Shelley, true moral behaviour is to be found in the social sphere as this is the sphere which is defined by justice and social duty; these are issues which, in a somewhat more conservative fashion, are debated in **Dracula**. Shelley, however, is not solely concerned with debunking Romantic Idealism, she is also concerned with exploring the ambiguities which are, for her, inherent to desire. This is specifically shown in the relations between Victor and the monster and Victor and his family. Shelley's account of desire is inevitably a version of events, but it is an interesting one because it breaks with both Radcliffe's covert sense of desire and Lewis' exaggerated masculine version of it. In **Frankenstein**, desire appears to echo Freud's account of the unconscious and so bears relevance to how desire is constructed in **Dracula**.

In the opening of chapter five we see Victor's realisation of what he has created. The monster is not the perfect aesthetic object which his constitutional parts had suggested he would become. Victor, eventually worn out by feelings of disappointment, falls asleep and has a dream which involves both his fiancée, Elizabeth, and his dead mother. Victor's account is that:-

> I thought I saw Elizabeth, in the bloom of health, walking in the streets of Ingolstadt. Delighted and surprised, I embraced her, but as I imprinted the first kiss on her lips, they became livid with the hue of death; her features appeared to change, and I thought that I held the corpse of my dead mother in my arms; a shroud enveloped her form, and I saw the grave worms crawling in the folds of the flannel. (p.106).

Here we can see that Victor's ambivalence towards Elizabeth operates at an unconscious level. He gives Elizabeth the kiss of death and turns her (in an Oedipal fashion) into another ambivalent object of desire, his mother. What is significant about this is that it is associated with the dream (10). The unconscious plays a foundational role in **Frankenstein** which is later echoed by texts such as Stevenson's **The Strange Case of Dr Jekyll and Mr Hyde** and Stoker's **Dracula**.

Victor awakens and escapes from the monster, about whom he tells Walton, "'No mortal could support the horror of that countenance. A mummy again endued with animation could not be so hideous as that wretch'"(p.106).

A striking feature of the Gothic is the similarity which it bears to the dream, in particular how, like the dream, it is a cryptic form which is often characterised by the use of bad puns. Here we can see how Victor's description of the monster takes on a wider significance than the purely aesthetic if we keep in view the Gothic tendency to use puns. The real horror here, so soon after the dream of holding his dead mother, is signalled by the reference to "'A mummy again endued with animation'". A familiar Gothic fear, the return of the dead is referred to in the monster's own physical make up. The implication therefore is that in Victor's mind, as revealed through the connection between his dream and his account of the monster's "'countenance'", Elizabeth, his mother and the monster are related.

This becomes clear later on in the novel when we see that it is the monster who craves the world of social (and sexual) intercourse from which Victor is fleeing. The monster, ironically, is granted the type of social isolation which Victor is envious of; this suggests that the monster and Victor are connected at an unconscious level. This argument is one established by Mary Poovey (11) who points out that the monster's killing of Victor's family literalises Victor's own figurative killing of them when he isolates himself at Inglostadt. This is also underlined by the reluctance with which Victor returns to his family. After the death of his brother, William, Justine Moritz and Henry Clerval, Victor makes the following incriminating outburst to his father, "'- I murdered her, William, Justine, and Henry - they all died by my hands'"(p.229). His father remonstrates with Victor and regards this view as the product of Victor's delirium; Victor replies "'I am not mad[...]the sun and the heavens who have viewed my operations, can bear witness of my truth. I am the assassin of those most innocent victims; they died by my machinations'"(p.230). This might appear to be an expression of Victor's sense of guilt about what his creation has done, however such a view does not explain why it is that Victor is so eager to apportion blame to himself unless at some level there is a connection between himself and the monster. This means that what the novel suggests is that the monster enacts out Victor's unconscious wishes; Victor is thereby simultaneously damned on two levels, the social and the psychological.

In looking at Radcliffe, Lewis and here Mary Shelley we can see how there is a development in ideas concerning the subject, at least the subject as it is constructed in Gothic texts. In Radcliffe's writings the heroes and heroines are granted a virtuous sensibility which enables them to indulge in the pleasures offered by the sublime. This is a double edged experience because although the sublime confirms the subject (suggests their virtue) it is at the expense of losing a grasp upon the social world, a world which leads her heroines into difficulties in the first place. With Lewis it is the case that 'natural' male sexuality requires appropriate outlets or else it will manifest itself in twisted ways. For Mary Shelley there is a psychological plane which dramatises Victor's complex responses towards the social world. All three writers share the similarity that they posit the existence of apparently intangible realities, the sublime, desire, and the unconscious. It is this reliance upon an idea of the intangible which marks out the Gothic idiom and bears relevance for a reading of **Dracula**.

Dracula works through similar recognisable traits as these writers but in a way which gives them a particular turn by focusing them around ideas of sex and sexuality. I will return to this in chapters two and three. Before moving on to discuss **Dracula** in detail it is important to explore some theories of the Gothic and to see why it is that a Freudian version of events is considered relevant to a wider understanding of its form.

The Critics

As I suggested earlier, one of the defining features of the Gothic is its sense of ambivalence. This ambivalence can take on many forms, it can be about authority, class, sexuality, and identity (amongst other things). It is important to see how the Gothic either undermines traditional views or celebrates them and to do this it is necessary to explore the moments of ambivalence to be found in Gothic texts. In **The Italian**, for example, there is a sense that in the character of Schedoni it privileges a Catholic notion of redemption, whereas the general flow of the novel is anti-Catholic (its demonisation of organised Catholic religion). The Gothic is prone to making these contradictions and we therefore have to acknowledge the inherent complexity of the form. In this section I will outline some theories of the Gothic in order to show how critics have regarded these moments of contradiction and to give some sense of where Gothic scholarship lies.

It is the post-Freudian legacy of criticism which I will focus upon here. The two books which I will discuss are important ones although to some degree introductory. They are David Punter's **The Literature of Terror** (1978) and Rosemary Jackson's **Fantasy: The Literature of Subversion** (1981)(12). Both are to some degree authoritative because they take into account the preceding tradition of Gothic criticism as well as formulating their own set of observations on the form. Punter's book is the more historical of the two looking at, as its subtitle indicates 'A history of Gothic Fictions from 1765 to the Present Day'.

Jackson's book is more overtly theoretical and is divided into two parts. The first part is an outline of existing theories of the Gothic and a rigorous attempt to construct a way of reading the Gothic. The second part is a somewhat cursory attempt to analyse Gothic texts ranging from Walpole's **The Castle of Otranto** (1765) to contemporary writers such as Thomas Pynchon. This second part is overly ambitious due to a lack of space and does not really do justice to the form other than implicitly acknowledge its diversity.

In exploring their accounts I will focus upon their construction of a theory of the Gothic, rather than replicate their historical insights concerning specific texts.

It is in chapter fifteen of **The Literature of Terror** that Punter outlines his version of the Gothic, which for him is a form which is dominated by three features, paranoia, barbarism, and taboo. Paranoia is manifested in the Gothic through its use of ambiguity which means that the Gothic is often uncertain about the judgements which it makes. This uncertainty suggests that things are inherently unstable, so that issues such as class, society, and sexuality are problematised. This is, for Punter, potentially a radical feature of the Gothic because it indicates that cultural 'certainties' are open to negotiation. His second marker, that of barbarism, is linked to how the Gothic returns to an apparently savage past. This is something which can be observed through the Gothic's frequent reconstruction of feudal pasts in decline, and can be found in vampire stories that express a 'fear of the aristocracy' (p.405). This is a point which I will develop further when I discuss Punter's account of the historical climate which produced the Gothic. The third point, taboo, is broadly linked, although Punter does not say so, to the potentially subversive ends of paranoia. In taboo, areas of life '[...]which are generally swept under the carpet in the interests of social and psychological equilibrium' are expressed (p.405).

These three definitions are helpful ones through which to approach the Gothic, although it might appear that they construct an uneasy alliance between psychoanalytical and historical readings. However, although the Gothic is more complex than this Punter's version of paranoia is defined by determining historical contexts, and it is important to note that the types of anxieties to be found in the Gothic are historical as well as psychological ones. One obvious feature of the Gothic is the fashion in which it handles the 'unreal'. This is not solely indicated by thematic content it is also indicated by often convoluted narrative forms, as in **Frankenstein** and the multi-vocal structure of **Dracula**, for example. The effect of this is to highlight the status which writing has within the text. What the Gothic is opposed to is not simply the Realist novel but rather the techniques which are used in the Realist novel in order to lull the reader into accepting the social veracity of it own unreal (fictional) world. There is a dilemma involved in this because:-

> Gothic fiction[...]finds itself operating between two structural poles. On the one hand, because it rejects

the account which realism gives of the world, it seeks to express truth through the use of other modes and genres[...]in order to demonstrate that the individual's involvement with the world is not merely linear, but is composed of moments with resonances and depths which can only be captured through the disruptive power of extensive metaphor and symbolism. On the other hand, because the Gothic writer does not want his(sic) writing to be construed as 'mere' fantasy, it becomes important to establish its validity within the text itself.
(pp.408-9).

What is therefore required is a Coleridgean suspension of disbelief which will pull the ideal reader into the Gothic's impossible world. It achieves this through a variety of techniques, some of them formal, such as the found document, and some more complex, such as the construction of psychologically plausible responses. What Punter also identifies in the above quotation is the way that the Gothic is defined by hesitation, this is a hesitation between the real and the unreal and is something which is inscribed in the very ambiguity of the form. This ambiguity is present both in the fashion in which issues are debated and in the development of the form itself. The reason for this latter ambiguity is because, for Punter, the Gothic is essentially a middle class form of writing in its historical origins. The paradox is that the Gothic often subverts the mores of this particular class, leading Punter to the conclusion that, 'The central contradiction[...]from which all the others flow, is this: that Gothic can at one and the same time be categorised as a middle-class and as an anti-middle-class literature'(p.423).

Punter discusses changes in the eighteenth-century which resulted in the creation of a laissez-faire economy. Such an economy gave capitalism a certain maturity (due to maritime expansion) and resulted in the formulation of bourgeois individualism. However, this stress upon the individual brings with it new anxieties because it is assumed that they share the same set of values as that of the market place (individual 'freedom' as the freedom to make money). For Punter, this meant that writers began to consider 'whether there was in fact an essential contradiction between social values and the values of the individual'(p.415). This is the contradiction which generates middle-class writing which appears to be critical of middle-class values.

So then, for Punter the Gothic's ambiguity can be related to the ambivalent position which a particular class found itself in during the eighteenth-century. In Punter's account there is this historical account of the form's origin which exists alongside his identification of its specific thematic features.

Punter, when discussing the dominant issues to be found in the Gothic makes the claim that, 'Gothic fiction is erotic at root: it knows that to channel sexual activity into narrow confines of conventionality is repressive and, in the end, highly dangerous' (p.411). Punter here perhaps too readily accepts a basically Freudian version of events (indicated also in his use of taboo), but what it does gesture towards is the peculiar way in which the Gothic articulates desire. The Gothic rarely expresses desire in an overt way but instead tends to use symbol and metaphor in order to cloak its excesses. This means that to understand how desire is used it is necessary for us to decode it and so breakdown its discretions. The Gothic does not always suggest that repression is a bad thing, Radcliffe versus Lewis for example, but it does mean that issues concerning sexuality appear to be ever present.

To conclude on Punter. His three registers of paranoia, barbarism, and taboo offer a reasonable way in which to approach a Gothic text. These registers are also appropriate ones through which to look at **Dracula**. Stoker's novel evidences a persecution paranoia (see Harker's opening journal), a fear of an aristocratic, feudal, past expressed as a fear of barbarism (the danger that the modern world could 'regress'), and it also deals in issues associated with taboo, most notably that of polymorphous sexuality. Also, Punter's historical account of the rise of the Gothic is convincing and enables us to locate the contradictory nature of the Gothic to specific cultural anxieties. These anxieties create ambivalence because 'Gothic fiction demonstrates the *potential* of revolution by daring to speak the socially unspeakable; but the very act of speaking it is an ambiguous gesture' (p.417). The ambivalence being that the form appears to attack middle-class lifestyles whilst simultaneously celebrating them. This is not to suggest that the Gothic is in any way escapist but rather that it conceals (through metaphor and symbol, for example) its assault on particular mores. Punter's view is suggestive here but one issue which he consistently fails to take into account is related to the labelling of 'evil'.

Rosemary Jackson in **Fantasy: The Literature of Subversion** examines how definitions of evil are often deployed in Gothic texts in order to reaffirm conservative political positions, she writes 'Any social order tends to exclude as 'evil' anything radically different from itself or which threatens it with destruction, and this conceptualisation, this naming of difference as evil, is a significant ideological gesture'(p.52). It is this naming of evil which helps to clarify some of the ambiguities to be found in the Gothic. **Dracula**, for example, on one level implies that something is wrong with a society which represses apparently 'natural' urges. In this way society is cast as the villain and the novel offered a Victorian readership the vicarious experience of an unbounded sexuality. This experience of the reader happens at a covert level because the novel utilises many of the symbolic devices, identified by Punter, in order to conceal its sexual content. However, what such a reading overlooks is where the definition of 'evil' lies in all of this. It is the Count who is inherently evil and as such it is his symbolic sexual promiscuity which is triumphed over at the end, rather than society for supposedly repressing this promiscuity; this means that the novel is not quite as sexually radical as it might at first appear.

However, this idea of a defining concept of evil is one which can only be reasonably applied in the final instance. For much of **Dracula** it is indeed the case that the novel flirts with the socially 'unacceptable' and although this might be given a conservative resolution it does suggest that there is something missing from contemporary experience. As Jackson puts it '[...]fantasy characteristically attempts to compensate for a lack resulting from cultural constraints; it is a literature of desire, which seeks that which is experienced as absence and loss'(p.3). This inevitably returns us to Punter's idea that the Gothic is founded upon contradiction. The Gothic might attempt to expel that which is subversive but only after it has explored the limits of cultural constraints.

Jackson is more concerned with how the Gothic transgresses boundaries than Punter she looks at similar ideas of taboo but is not concerned, with any real precision, with historical specifics. That is not to say that she does not acknowledge the role which history has in forming texts, but rather that her sympathies lean towards the psychoanalytical. This is perhaps not surprising, Punter also acknowledges that the Gothic is fundamentally concerned with explorations of the erotic. One of Jackson's main claims is that, 'In its broadest sense, fantastic literature has always been concerned with revealing and exploring the interrelations of the 'I' and the 'not-I', of self and other'(p.53). This means that she regards the fantastic (which includes the Gothic) as a form which explores what it means to be 'human', and the Gothic does this by positing the existence of inhuman forms, vampires, devils, ghosts, monsters and so on. Jackson's argument is that our ideas concerning humanity are ideological ones (notions of our humanity tending to be used in order to regulate or 'naturalise' behaviour), and the Gothic becomes a privileged space in which these assumptions are debated. This is linked to the 'ideological gesture' which is associated with defining the non-human as evil. Some novels explore this definition, **Frankenstein**, for example, explodes the idea that definitions of evil are relevant to secular circumstances. This is worth bearing in mind when contrasting a writer with religious leanings such as Radcliffe, and one for whom religion is merely a structural device such as Stoker, which is indicated in his representation of Van Helsing's inept quasi-Catholicism. Jackson writes:-

> [...]whereas a religious subject has faith that a sense of unbeing, a dissolution of the ego, will lead to ultimate unity with a devine beloved, a sceptical, atheistic subject has no such faith. In the place of transcendent ideals, there is discovered a zero point, a space of non-being, an absence. (p.78).

This absence is discovered in the social order because what is truly "discovered" is the way that desire is kept in check by that social order. For Jackson then, the post-Romantic Gothic is characterised by the centrality which it gives to desire, in this the emphasis is both upon the subject (the desires they are subject to) and society (how it tries to police desire). For this reason Jackson privileges a psychoanalytical reading of the Gothic because the Gothic subject, like the Freudian patient, is prone to fears and desires which they cannot fully comprehend (because society will not allow full comprehension).

The links between the Gothic and a largely Freudian version of psychoanalysis are not just suggested by structural similarities. There also exists an historical underpinning of changes in subjectivity which are similarly mapped out in fiction as they are in psychoanalysis. It is therefore not coincidental that the late nineteenth-century Gothic overtly explores issues of displaced desire and that this is also the period which culminates in Freud's **The Interpretation of Dreams**.

Although Jackson favours the psychoanalytical there is an acknowledgement that the Other (vampire, ghost, monster and so on) is not a purely psychological projection. The form which the Other takes is also inflected by cultural preoccupations, '[...]it is the identification, the naming of otherness, which is a telling index of a society's religious and political beliefs'(p.52). A Gothic monster (as in **Frankenstein** or **Dr Jekyll and Mr Hyde** for example) might well bear some relation to the rebellious force of the Id, but it is necessary to move beyond this and ask why the monstrous takes on these precise forms. This is also a productive way in which to integrate a psychoanalytical perspective with an historical-cultural approach.

I have discussed Punter and Jackson here because although there are different emphases in their work there also exist some important parallels. One shared claim concerns the importance which is attached to the historical forces which produce particular texts. This enables us to account for changes in the use of certain Gothic symbols over an historical period. Psychoanalysis would appear to lend itself to an investigation of the Gothic because like the Gothic it too is concerned with accounts of the irrational and versions of desire. Punter's and Jackson's are not the only approaches to the Gothic but they offer useful and lucid introductions to the core issues which characterise the Gothic form.

In the next chapter I will explore **Dracula** in some detail. Whilst it is worth bearing in mind the views of critics such as Punter and Jackson, I will take a somewhat different tack. I will explore how the novel constructs a version of desire and I will link this to aspects of victorian culture. I will make these connections by reading the novel through the French historian of ideas, Michel Foucault. Foucault's **The History of Sexuality** (vol I) is an account of victorian sexuality which has a direct bearing on many of the issues to be found in Stoker's novel.

Chapter Two-Sex and Text; The Problem of 'Truth' in Dracula.

Introduction

In this chapter I will approach **Dracula**(1) through the work of Michel Foucault. Foucault's accounts of the employment of disciplinary procedures and the effects which they have upon the body forms a helpful starting-point from which to look at the Gothic. Foucault's concern with the regularisation of bodies, their movements, desires, and secrets can be found in his accounts of institutional power in **Madness and Civilisation** and **Discipline and Punish**. These ideas are also to be found in his account of Victorian sexuality in **The History of Sexuality** (vol I)(2); which I will refer to extensively here. It is worth keeping in mind that Foucault is less concerned with the supposedly controlling moves of ideology than are more Marxist orientated critics. For Foucault there are moments of resistance to power which suggests that an ideologically controlled view of things is compromised; it is these moments of resistance which we can also see occurring in Stoker's novel. Before discussing **Dracula** in detail I will outline Foucault's understanding of Victorian sexuality and what it is that this sexuality is contrasted with.

For Foucault, what characterises Victorian sexuality is a **Scientia Sexualis, or a science** of sexuality. This sexuality is effectively policed by particular practices (most of them psychoanalytical ones) which attempt to gauge the 'health' of the individual. It is these practices which characterise the emergence of the bourgeoisie because for them power is assured by the maintenance of healthy lines of descent. Money and therefore power, is passed down to generations who can sustain a middle-class position. The bourgeois subject is bourgeois because they possess a certain wealth. In order to ensure that these lines of descent do not becomes corrupted the scientific emphasis becomes placed upon sexuality and what it means to possess a 'healthy' sexuality. This means that sex is something which required scrutinisation, and which in turn leads to the construction of a set of supposedly aberrant sexual behaviours such as homosexuality and masturbation, for example. It is these alleged 'aberrations' which undermine the ideal of a 'healthy' heterosexuality which guarantees the possibility of familial descent. Also, sex became scrutinised for any possible diseases which might inhere to it; the idea of disease here is not so much a bodily one as one defined by a moral outlook. Foucault writes that '[...]not only could sex be effected by its own diseases, it could also, if it was not controlled, transmit diseases or create others that would afflict future generations'(p.118). From this it is possible to conclude that such examinations were not solely concerned with identifying physical 'impurities' but moral ones as well. It is this idea of a science of sexuality which Foucault contrasts with what he terms an **Ars Erotica**, which is a type of sexual expression which is identified with Feudal or Aristocratic culture. This **Ars Erotica** is therefore associated with a time when possession of a certain kind of blood was considered important. An aristocrat is an aristocrat because they possess aristocratic blood (a circular argument which, as we will see later, also applies to the vampire; a vampire is a vampire because they possess the blood of the vampire). This means that the erasure of apparently congenital aberrations is not so important with the aristocracy because their status has a permanence which the bourgeoisie does not have (George III's 'madness' for example did not stop him from functioning as the King).

For Foucault, the bourgeoisie's sexuality was necessarily a precarious one because it was subject to disease and infection, the way to gain access to it was through 'the slow surfacing of confidential statements'(p.63). There thus existed a pressure to confess this sexuality which in part entailed a relaxation of the bounds of sexual secrecy. Foucault quotes from Alfonso de' Ligouri's **Preceptes sur Le Sixieme Commandement** which was translated in to French in 1835, Ligouri states that the subject should 'Tell everything[...]not only consummated acts, but sensual touchings, all impure gazes, all obscene remarks[...]all consenting thoughts'(p.21). For Foucault such remarks are typically associated with the compulsion to confess in the Catholic faith. It is out of this specific religious scene that modern (Freudian) psychoanalysis emerges; it too is associated with a compulsion to tell (known as the talking cure).

According to Foucault, the bourgeoisie considered its sexuality to be a fragile secret that had to be discovered at all costs'(pp.120-1). This also means that the problem of sexuality was associated with a problem of 'truth', a science was created which regularised peoples' statements and controlled the fashion in which those statements could be made.

These descriptions of the changes and developments in sexuality bear relevance to a reading of **Dracula**. In the novel we can see that there exists an antagonism between a system which is defined by a symbolics of blood (The symbolism of the significance of blood for the aristocracy) and a system which is defined by a science of the subject (the opposing bourgeois group). I will argue that the Count threatens the bourgeoisie with extinction because it is through his method of infection that he moves Lucy (and nearly Mina) outside of the realms of 'acceptable' bourgeois codes of sexual behaviour. Also we can see in the novel how characters such as Van Helsing and Dr Seward operate as nascent psychoanalysts, with the former stressing the importance of disclosing personal information. The novel largely consists of a number of personal documents such as letters and diaries which are examined by members of the group who are looking for the hidden clues which can be found concerning the Count.

An Outline of the Argument

The part of the novel which I will examine first is Harker's opening account of his experiences at

Castle Dracula. This is an important testimony because it is its apparently implausible circumstances which later accounts authenticate. What constitutes the 'truth' is at issue here, and it is this notion of there existing a verifiable 'truth' which I later explore in relation to the novel's descriptions of sexual desire. What this first scene also suggests is that writing is an important factor here; texts have to be verified according to directions which are the same as those applied to sexuality, this is a point which I will later elaborate upon. I will also examine the 'seduction' of Lucy in some detail because this is the clearest example in the novel of how a character is absorbed by the Count's sexuality. I therefore examine the process through which the possession of a certain type of blood leads to the possession of the body and its sexuality. I follow this with an exploration of the representation of the Count's body; of how it is that his body is defined through contemporary accounts of criminality (specifically through the ideas of Lombroso) which has the effect of making the Count visible (and so decodable) despite his frequent absences.

The problem of what constitutes 'truth' is made apparent early on in the novel as we see Harker's (western) sense of certainty becoming eroded. He cannot even be sure of the exact location of Castle Dracula itself because, 'I was not able to light on any map or work giving the exact locality of the Castle Dracula, as there are no maps of this country as yet to compare with our own Ordinance Survey maps'(p.10). Such an apparently innocent

Harker

comment signals the way that Harker judges normalcy in western ways, it is these judgements which become compromised as he confronts an eastern culture where these judgements do not apply. Harker again suggests this when he writes the seemingly bald statement that 'It seems to me that the further East you go the more unpunctual are the trains'(p.11). The implication here is that Harker is entering a world in which irrationality and mystery reign (things becoming imprecise). Harker initially tries to assimilate this 'strange' environment through an idea of the picturesque, in this way he operates as a tourist who takes notes of particular recipes (for Mina's benefit) and who regards the local land-workers as adding colour to his experience of this strange terrain. Harker also readily dismisses the fear which the locals express when he announces his destination. This apparently benign country where the peasants are 'very harmless and rather wanting in natural self-assertion'(p.11) is later to reveal a more sinister side to it which Harker is unable to explain away.

These opening pages of the novel direct us towards the idea that Harker's strictly western sense of his own rationality will be inadequate when he is confronted by that which usurps his sense of a 'natural' law (it is therefore relevant that his occupation is one concerned with issues of legality). What Harker comes to realise in his confrontations at Castle Dracula is that history appears to be oddly out of synchronisation. He is prepared to accept that the Count is an aging aristocrat, but what he cannot accept is the idea that a feudal past can carry on into the modern world. Harker writes of his situation that 'It is nineteenth century up-to-date with a vengeance. And yet, unless my senses deceive me, the old centuries had, and have, powers of their own which mere 'modernity' cannot kill'(p.49). This directs us to a central crux of the novel which is that a major threat is that the past can take over the present and in doing so would destroy the bourgeois values associated with the opposing group.

In **Dracula** dead history is brought back to life. The Count is necessarily Other to Harker because of this historicisation of his own past which overlaps with the modern world. Dracula resurrects dead history (the history of the Wallachians and Saxons) and in doing so grants a modern status to his aristocracy. Dracula tells Harker that '"[...]in our veins flows the blood of many brave races who fought as the lion fights, for lordship"'(p.41). Historically, the Count is situated at the point where the bourgeoisie emerge (he is seemingly an aristocrat in decline). The Count's feudal past is the background against which the bourgeoisie arrive, but it is also a system which excludes bourgeois sensibility. Feudalism is only 'safe' as long as it has been confined to the past, a confinement which the Count undermines. Chris Baldick writes in **In Frankenstein's Shadow: Myth, Monstrosity and Nineteenth Century Writing** that 'Dracula is feudalism's death warmed up'(p.148).

This historical displacement of the Count and his subsequent clash with the opposing bourgeois group is identified in the novel as a clash between bodies (the 'healthy' bourgeois body versus the infecting, debased, body of the vampire). There is also a conflict which I suggested earlier, between textuality and non-textuality. The Count's body is associated with a variety of impossible characteristics such as its precarious immortality, its reformation into animal shape, and its peculiar functions. Harker, for example, watches the Count leave his room and scale head downwards down the castle wall; Harker comments 'What manner of man is this, or what manner of creature is it in the semblance of man?'(p.47). We are told that the Count is thin but yet he possesses 'the strength of twenty men'(p.283). His body thus transgresses certain rules of possibility, but it is subject to other laws. The crucifix, an inability to cross water unaided, and garlic, all function as alternative prohibitions upon the vampire's body. These alternative restraints do not however reveal the source of the most immediate clash between Dracula and the opposing group which is defined as a clash between sexual bodies. It is here that Foucault's definition of an **Ars Erotica** which opposes a **Scientia Sexualis** becomes relevant. It is the Count who embodies the first form and the opposing group the latter. Foucault writes that the **Ars Erotica** functioned through a process in which:-

> [...]the relationship to the master who holds the secrets, is of paramount importance; and only he, working alone, can transmit this art in an esoteric manner and as the culmination of an initiation in which he guides the disciple's progress with unfailing skill and severity(p.32).

The Count creates disciples, propagates his system, by infecting blood. This contrasts with the idea that it is a 'healthy' sexuality which controls descent. When Mina, for example, recounts her 'seduction' she writes that the Count said to her '"[...]you, their best beloved one, are now to me flesh of my flesh; blood of my blood; kin of my kin"'(p.343). Here the Count makes a claim that he has successfully absorbed Mina, in doing so the danger is that she ceases to be fully bourgeois; her own sexuality could take on the guise of a secretive **Ars Erotica** rather than an exposed sexuality which can be analysed by a **Scientia Sexualis**. What this comment by the Count therefore points to is the way that he can eradicate the bourgeoisie by absorbing them through his own power. This is something which Van Helsing acknowledges when he states that '"[...]to fail here is not mere life or death. It is that we become as him[...]"'(p.284).

So then, the Count is defined as irrevocably Other because of the way in which he historicises his own body, '"What devil or what witch was ever so great as Attila, whose blood is in these veins?"'(p.41). The Count is both historically and physically impossible; his strength, his ability to metamorphose into a wolf or a bat reveals his 'unnatural' expression of nature, or more radically the challenge which he presents to Harker's assumptions about nature. It is the Count's sexuality which threatens to absorb members of the bourgeois group which would condemn them to an endless repetition (vampirism repeats itself over and over again in the search for new 'converts'). What all of this means is that sexuality in the novel is closely related to the formation of the subject. The novel suggests that the 'truth' of the subject is defined by the 'truth' of their sexuality. It is the Count who poses a problem of truth for the bourgeois group because '[...]sex was constituted as a problem of truth' (Foucault, p.56) in **Scientia Sexualis**. The Count's subjectivity (sexuality) differs from the bourgeois group's because of its erotic connotations and through his non-textuality.

Textualiy

The bourgeois group are most frequently made present to us through their diary accounts. The effect of this is that they appear to be self-present through a series of dramatic monologues; however, most of these accounts are written after the event which means that the world is to some degree reified (is already given) and that they are passive observers of what has already happened. Also, their accounts are personal, sometimes secret, texts. Francis Barker has written of the diary form that within it there is, '[...]the apparent ease of its discourse, launched from an inner place to an outer, clarified world; the guilty secret not only of its writing but of its sexuality"(p.11)(3), because '[...]the bourgeois subject substitutes for its corporal body the rarefied body of the text'(p.62). In contrast to this the feudal Count has no text, his desire is only present to the extent that we see it manifested through those he has infected. His subjectivity is a non-bourgeois one and is therefore not associated with the historical rise of the diarist. The Count is an object, rather than a subject, of discourse; he does not self-reflect, he does not appear in the mirror.

As I suggested earlier, the most important text in **Dracula** is that of Harker's opening journal. It is the secrets of that text which the other texts unravel and so give it the status of 'truth'. This support for the claims of his journal is also an attempt to prop-up his own particular attempts to gain a scientific perspective on the events surrounding him; they are an attempt to give credence to his claim that he can '[...]begin with facts - bare meagre facts, verified by books and figures, and of which there can be no doubt'(p.42). It is this idea of how to verify which is so important to the novel because the Count is 'un-dead', he is an impossible being, whose status as an object of verifiable knowledge is only present as an absence within the scientific discourse of Van Helsing and Dr Seward. This failure on the part of scientific practice is identified by Van Helsing as signalling a deficiency within that practice, he tells Seward '"[...]it is the fault of our science that it wants to explain all; and if it explains not, then it says there is nothing to explain"'(p.229).

It is not however science which solely destroys the Count, it is also a circulation of texts which forms a joined narration which forces members of the group outside of their narrative positions. This effectively transforms them from being isolated observers (writers) into becoming participants (readers), which means that 'truth' is produced communally through the exchange of texts. It is

45

important also to note that the novel links this idea of a textuality which produces 'truth' to a wider frame which is associated with the 'truth' of sexuality. It is Van Helsing who confirms the veracity of Harker's journal telling Mina that, '"You may sleep without doubt. Strange and terrible as it is, it is true!"'(p.224). Harker on hearing this expresses his relief in terms which suggest that he regains sexual power, without this veracity he felt 'It was the doubt as to the reality of the whole thing that knocked me over. I felt impotent'(p.225). With truth assured sexuality itself becomes assured.

This scrutinisation of writing is located in the novel as being a moral imperative, it is Van Helsing who tells Seward, when handing over the collected accounts, '"What is here told[...]may be the beginning of the end to you and me and many another; or it may sound the knell of the Un-Dead[...]"'(p.262). Their collected texts therefore contain crucial information. Seward observes that when Mina and Jonathan have collected this material '[...]they will be able to show a whole connected narrative'(p.269), they will therefore be able to tell the story of what has been happening to them in a meaningful way. This document is subject to interpretation and reinterpretation as the group struggle to find the latent clues which are hidden within it. Mina writes of this document, 'Whilst they are resting, I shall go over all carefully, and perhaps I may arrive at some conclusion. I shall try to follow the professor's example, and think without prejudice on the facts before me[...]'(p.416). It is these facts which have surfaced due to Van Helsing's encouragement, which sounds similar to the appeal made by Ligouri which I quoted earlier, he says to Seward, "'Nothing is too small, I counsel you, put down in record even your doubts and surmises'"(p.146). That which is apparently inconsequential "'too small'" is therefore given a wider significance, Van Helsing stresses that it has to appear in writing (has to become documentary evidence). This links to what Foucault regards as the compelling nature of the disclosure of sexuality with the bourgeoisie; he writes that '[...]sex became something to say, and to say exhaustively in accordance with deployments that were varied, but all, in their own way compelling'(p.32), there existed a '[...]polymorphous incitement to discourse'(p.34). It is these extracts from the novel which reveal that a similar 'incitement to discourse' has taken place.

It is this idea of the confessional nature of these disclosures which is important in the novel. Sometimes the 'truth' in such confessions is at such a latent level that it requires access to a character's subconscious. When Mina is infected by the Count, for example, she is hypnotised in order to enable entry into her subconscious mind; a subconscious in which there can be found important truths. The reason for this is that she functions as the missing link between the world of the group and the world of the Count. She is somewhat like Renfield who mimics the Count in an "'indexy kind of way'"(p.296). This use here of writing to describe the connection is revealing and is a type of description which is employed elsewhere in the novel. The Count, for example, is the '"[...]author of all this our sorrow[...]"'(p.260); he can only be destroyed when 'He is confined within the limitations of his earthly envelope'(p.348); all of this suggests that areas associated with writing are problematical, and they are problematical because writing is closely connected to notions of 'health'. Van Helsing, for example, towards the end of the novel regards Mina's lack of interest in writing in her diary as indicative of her infection, he notes that there '[...]the silence is now often; as so it was with Miss Lucy'(p.384), and 'She make no entry into her little diary, she who write so faithful at every pause'(p.431). It is this lack of interest in writing which indicates just how far Mina's infection has developed. It is important to note that this is bound-up with differing notions of subjectivity. That is to say that in the clash between an **Ars Erotica** and a **Scientia Sexualis**, there is also a clash taking place between different versions of subjectivity, between pre-bourgeois and bourgeois definitions of the self. Francis Barker writes that:-

> Pre-bourgeois subjection does not properly involve subjectivity at all, but a condition of dependent membership in which place and articulation are defined not by an interiorized self-recognition - complete or partial, percipient or unknowing[...]but by incorporation in the body politic, (p.31).

It is this absorption into a body 'politic' which closely resembles some of the features of **Ars Erotica**. Vampirism itself is a state in which 'dependent membership' controls and in which the idea of self-recognition (the basis on which self-reflection can occur) is obviated by duty to the 'master'.

The most overt example of this process of absorption can be found in the descriptions of the 'seduction' of Lucy Westerna. In her account to Mina of her dream (an account of her seduction) it is blood which plays an important part. Blood is the taste of the 'something' which is 'very sweet and very bitter'(p.121) that surrounds her; and it is the dream which overpowers her in a directly (but crudely) symbolically sexual way, i.e. the phallic 'West lighthouse was right under me'(p.121). Seward tests Lucy's blood for impurities, however, '"The qualitive analysis gives a quite normal condition[...]"'(p.136); this leads Seward to believe that her problem might be mental rather than physical. Blood is also defined by who has ownership of it (blood being seen as the key to identity). The Count corrupts Lucy by taking her blood and by introducing 'moral' impurities. For this process to be halted it is necessary that Lucy's blood should be replaced from a 'healthy' source (so that she can be penetrated in a 'healthy' fashion. The first transfusion is from her fiancé Holmwood, who is '"[...]so young and strong and of blood so pure[...]"'(p.149), which signals that beneath this supposedly scientific procedure there exists a sexual hierarchy which determines priority of access to Lucy. After Lucy has received this transfusion she re-enters the world of written language, writing that 'Arthur feels very, very close to me. I seem to feel his presence warm about me'(p.154). Lucy effectively loses any real sense of her own identity after this point. There is none of her own blood left, it is either replaced by the Count's or by the group's, this means that her identity is only secured to the extent that she is absorbed through the blood of others. There is an irony in this because the group have unwittingly become vampiric by 'infecting' Lucy's body, but in a fashion which accords with their notions of the 'healthy'. These transfusions are a disguised sexual act, they are a 'healthy' form of penetration. The second transfusion is with Seward, who recounts his experience as '[...]the draining away of one's blood, no matter how willingly it be given, is a terrible feeling-'(p.156). It is not the loss of his own blood here which is the 'terrible feeling', it is the guilty symbolic penetration of Lucy's body by one who has had his marriage proposal to lucy rejected; revealingly Van Helsing warns Seward not to tell Holmwood of this second transfusion as it may '"enjealous him,"'(p.156). Another transfusion is with Morris, who had also had his marriage proposal rejected, and another is with Van Helsing.

With these transfusions completed there is a further irony. It is because this medical procedure is a coded moment of penetration that Lucy has now fulfilled one of her earlier aspirations, which was a desire for promiscuity. She had previously written to Mina concerning her three marriage proposals that 'Why can't they let a girl marry three men, or as many as want her,[...] But this is heresy, and I must not say it'(p.76). Lucy's subsequent transformation into the Bloofar Lady would appear to offer her the opportunity to enact out this desire in a more active form, we learn that her 'purity' had changed 'to voluptuous wantonness' (pp.252-3). However, this transformation results in Lucy inverting the suckling relationship between mother and child (4) rather than making her sexually active. She thus appears to invert the maternalism which the novel will valorise at the end in the scene with Mina and her child. It is Mina who is described as possessing a healthy form of maternity, a maternity which the novel defines as a powerful inner force, Mina writes that 'We women have something of the mother in us that makes us rise above smaller matters when the mother-spirit is invoked' (p.275).

Lucy becomes restored to the bourgeois symbolic order through her phallic, ritualised, staking. It is this staking which turns Lucy into an object of 'healthy' sex, which means that the novel also tends to eroticise violence. We are told of Lucy that what signals her vampiric alteration is her 'unhealthy' sexualized appearance; she had 'seemed like a nightmare of Lucy as she lay there, the pointed teeth, the bloodstained, voluptuous mouth - which it made one shudder to see - the whole carnal and unspiritual appearance, seeming like a devilish mockery of Lucy's sweet purity'(p.256). The language also takes on sexual connotations, in an incidental description of a melting candle Seward describes how 'the sperm dropped' (p.236) onto Lucy's coffin. Lucy's staking, like that of the blood transfusions, also suggests that there exists rights of priority concerning access to her body. The task of the staking is passed to Holmwood, because it would be by '"the hand of him who loved her best"' (p.258). Inevitably Lucy's staking is described in terms of erotic abandonment:-

> The thing in the coffin writhed; and a hideous, blood-curdling screech came from the opened red lips. The body shook and quivered and twisted in wild contortions; the sharp white teeth champed together till the lips were cut and the mouth was smeared with a crimson foam. But Arthur never faltered. He looked like a figure of Thor as his untrembling arm rose and fell, driving deeper and deeper the mercy-bearing stake, whilst the blood from the pierced heart welled and spurted up around it. His face was set, and high duty seemed to shine through it; the sight of it gave us courage, so that our voices seemed to ring through the little vault (pp.258-9).

Here Lucy's 'opened red lips' and frothing mouth symbolically echo vaginal orgasm (in a representation familiar to post-Freudian readers, one of displacement upwards), with Holmwood 'driving deeper and deeper'. This is all carried out as if it were a crusade (rather than sexually sinister) as Holmwood is cheered on by the watching group, and so Lucy's body is violated in a way which, strangely, renders it healthy. Lucy is now no longer suspended between life and death, is no longer one of the undead; rather she is returned to an idea of a natural communality in death which is the symbolic erasure of her individuality. The psychoanalyst Jessica Benjamin has written that 'Death means continuity, in death, not life, each individual is united with the rest, sunk back into a sea of nondifferentiation' (5). Lucy is 'freed' from her vampirism through death, it is a 'natural' death (or so implicitly the novel wants us to believe) that is privileged here, which removes Lucy from suspension between an unnatural life and death.

The Count's Body

This sexualized nature of the staking of Lucy is one which is absent from the description of the Count's staking. He is stabbed and his body crumbles into dust, although it too shows 'a look of peace' (p.447) which is similar to that found on Lucy. This description is a brief one in the novel, but it should be noted that it is the Count's body (or an idea of it) which is the most striking one in the novel. His body, paradoxically, possesses an incorporeal corporality which is anchored in two ways. One is through notions of physiognomy which are derived from the nineteenth century criminologist, Lombroso. The other is evolutionary, whereby the Count is deemed to have not yet arrived at full maturity and as such is relatively weak; this second anchor is linked to the first via a discourse of criminality. To take the first point concerning Lombroso. Leonard Woolf in **Annotated Dracula** makes the following juxtapositions between descriptions of the Count given by Harker and descriptions of the criminal given by Lombroso:-

> Harker: 'His face was aquiline, with high bridge of the thin nose and peculiarly arched nostrils...'
> Lombroso: '(The criminal's) nose on the contrary...is often aquiline like the beak of a bird of prey.'

Harker: 'His eyebrows were very massive, almost meeting over the nose...'

Lombroso: 'The eyebrows are bushy and tend to meet across the nose.'

Harker: '...his ears were pale and at the tops extremely pointed.'

Lombroso: 'with a protuberance on the upper part of the posterior margin...a relic of the pointed ear...'(6).

The novel self-consciously points towards this idea of criminality when Mina says to Van Helsing '"The Count is a criminal and of criminal type, Nordau and Lombroso would so classify him"' (p.406). The Count is therefore identifiably criminal, this criminality is inscribed upon his features which means that he can be 'read'. The Count has no textual body, no account of his actions, but his physiognomy can be read as if it were a text. The Count's sexuality is what is latent in the others and it only appears when it has infected others and becomes an immediate problem which the group attempts to medically cure. It is the Count's own sexuality (his peculiar means of propagation through infection) which compromises the 'law' of sexuality which the group are attempting to uphold.

Foucault writes, '[...]the preoccupation with blood and the law has for nearly two centuries haunted the administration of sexuality' (p.149). It is the

Count's sexuality which is the inarticulate element in this. It is a from of sexuality which is decoded by the pseudo-scientific practice of Van Helsing.

The Count's physiognomy marks him out as being irredeemably criminal and this is not solely associated with his corrupting sexuality, but is also explicitly anchored through a notion of primivitism. The Count is described as possessing a child-like brain; Van Helsing says '"This criminal has not full man-brain"' (p.405) and that '"[...]he be not of man-stature as to brain. He is of child-brain in much"' (p.406). According to their contemporary ideas of evolution, the modern bourgeois group cannot be bested by that which has historically preceded it. However, it is the power of the Count, the potential strength of his brain, which is related to physical growth, suggesting that he too can evolve, '"[...]as his body keep strong and grow and thrive, so his brain grow too"' (p.380). It therefore becomes imperative that the Count is defeated before he gains full maturity, before he can become '"-the father or furtherer of a new order of beings, whose road must lead through Death, not Life"' (pp.359-60). The 'child' cannot be permitted to become 'the father' of 'a new order'. Like Lucy he has to be consigned to the only permitted form of non-textuality, which is death. The ultimate triumph of the group is the valorisation of its sexuality and the means through which it has achieved this, the circulation of their texts.

So, in Dracula there is a play of texts and bodies which implies that they are related. Foucault can be helpfully employed to identify how the novel works through a particular clash of sexualities. The task for the bourgeois group is to locate, read, and destroy the troublesome sexuality of the Count before it infects them all. It is the idea of writing in the novel which, I have been stressing, is a revealing one and it is this idea which I will explore in greater depth in the next section.

The Place of Writing

So far in this chapter I have looked at the connections which exist in **Dracula** between sexuality and textuality. However, it is important to note that the use of textuality is not necessarily an 'even' one in the novel because writing means different things at different times. There are three types of writing which I will briefly discuss here. They are those forms of writing which function as self-therapy, those which represent occasions which appear to obscure the action, and finally a specific moment when writing is explicitly linked to economics.

There exist moments in **Dracula** when writing is associated both with knowledge and with the possibility of self-therapy. The latter is apparent, for example, in Harker's opening journal when he writes '[...]I turn to my diary for repose. The habit of entering accurately must help to soothe me' (p.50). Later, Mina writes in a similar vein that '-I am anxious, and it soothes me to express myself here; it is like whispering to one's self and listening at the same time' (p.91). Later, Harker writes 'I must keep writing at every chance, for I dare not stop to think' (p.344). These instances reveal how writing is used as a means to externalise internal anxiety. The anxiety becomes distanced from the subject, and this is partly due to the social fashion in which writing is deployed throughout the novel. This is because the written text has implied readers in **Dracula**, which means that on a textual level the subject overcomes fears felt in isolation in order to transmit those fears at a communal level. It is a way of re-integrating the isolated subject into the 'conversation' of the novel.

Writing is also defined as inherently problematic because it functions in such a way that it obscures the action, this is because the act of writing takes the place of action. Harker's opening journal, for example, concludes with him seemingly imprisoned in Castle Dracula with no apparent means of escape. In the final scenes Harker hears the workmen removing the Count's coffins, Harker believes that when the men have left he will be killed by the three female vampires whom he had erotically encountered earlier. Harker, however, replaces action with an account of his predicament:-

> As I write there is in the passage below a sound of many tramping feet and the crash of weights being set down heavily, doubtless the boxes, with their freight of earth. There is a sound of hammering; it is the box being nailed down. Now I can hear the heavy feet tramping along the hall, with many other idle feet coming behind them (p.69).

Harker becomes a listener (Harker)/writer, and the reader is not informed of his means of escape. The implication in this is that the text is more important than lived 'reality'. We find this process echoed later on in the novel when Dr Seward is informed that Renfield has had a serious accident. This is how Dr Seward responds to this crisis:-

> The attendant came bursting into my room and told me that Renfield had somehow met with some accident. He had heard him yell; and when he went to him found him lying on his face on the floor, all covered with blood. I must go at once... (p.327).

Seward, of course does not 'go at once', first he writes it down. The implication in this is that experience has to be textually mediated in order for that experience to become 'truth'. It is this implication which ties it into the wider construction of writing in the novel that text and 'truth' are closely related. There is thus an anxiety, which we can see in the journalist's account of the arrival of the Demeter at Whitby, that experience might take '[...]place more quickly than it takes to write these words' (p.99). This means that temporality becomes another source of anxiety because there is the fear that actions can take place more quickly than they can be expressed. That which does not coincide with writing is therefore a threat to the group because it is through their texts that they are able to construct notions of a verifiable 'truth'.

Earlier, I stressed that the link between textuality and sexuality which is mediated through the form of a **Scientia Sexualis** was, historically, a bourgeois formation. It is because **Dracula** celebrates this bourgeois culture that it is not surprising to see an overt connection established between writing and money. This connection can be seen, for example, in Seward's account of Renfield before Renfield's fatal 'accident', here money and writing are explicitly linked in a fashion which echoes **Robinson Crusoe**. Seward writes of Renfield that:-

> He has evidently some deep problem in his mind, for he keeps a little note-book in which he is always jotting down something. Whole pages of it are filled with masses of figures, generally single numbers added up in batches, and then the totals added in batches again, as though he were 'focusing' some account, as the auditors put it (p.88).

It is this idea of money which Seward conflates with religion. After his marriage proposal to Lucy has been rejected, he writes of Renfield that:-

> He has closed the account most accurately, and to-day began a new record. How many of us begin a new record with each day of our lives?
> To me it seems only yesterday that my whole life ended with my new hope, and that truly I began a new record. So it will be until the Great Recorder sums me up and closes my ledger with a balance to profit or loss (p.90).

Writing then, is linked to money and to ethics (religion). The suggestion is that there exists a series of puns around the use of 'account' which variously refers to writing, to money, and to spoken confessions, and it is these connections which confirm and consolidate the bourgeois view of the novel.

Writing is therefore broken down into three discernable forms. There is the type of self-therapy which is embarked upon because it overcomes isolation. In another form we can see how it is that writing is elevated over action. This suggests that non-linguistic experiences are subservient to writing; in a wider sense this is connected to how Van Helsing attempts to banish desire from experience. In the third moment writing is likened to an account ledger with religious dimensions. It is these features which make the novel identifiable as riven by capitalist visions of society.

Conclusion

In this chapter I have looked at several features of **Dracula** which help to locate the novel within the context of Victorian culture. Specifically I have used Foucault's account of sexuality in order to show how the novel can be seen to be working through a set of similar dilemmas. His identification of a Victorian **Scientia Sexualis** is a helpful starting point which enables us to tie down the nebulous concept of desire to a particular historical and cultural moment. It is the sex of the bourgeoisie which is at issue here. Foucault sees this science of sexuality as operating to gauge the 'health' of the bourgeois subject. **Dracula** also evidences such a concern with the health of the subject as the group battles against the disease of vampirism. This vampirism involves an obvious paradox because it articulates the desire of the group anyway. This is manifested in Lucy's latent desire for promiscuity and her erotic dream, it is also present in Harker's own confession in his journal when he encounters the three female vampires, there he confesses that '"There was something about them that made me uneasy, some longing and at the same time some deadly fear. I felt in my heart a wicked, burning desire that they would kiss me with those red lips"' (p.51). It is this type of desire which the novel as a whole attempts to eradicate. It is by projecting their desire onto vampirism that it means that they can in turn be cured of 'impure' thoughts. In the final scene of the novel we learn that Jonathan and Mina's child is named after members of the group 'His bundle of names links all our little band of men together' (p.449); Carol A Senf has written about this scene that here, 'Individual sexual desire has apparently been so absolutely effaced that the narrators see this child as the result of their social union rather than the product of a sexual union between one man and one woman' (7). In effect sexuality has been equated with disease. What this suggests is the presence of repression in the novel, and it is not arbitrary that it is written in the century which culminates in the emergence of Freudian ideas, ideas which imply the possibility of a science of sexuality.

As Foucault has suggested, these ideas concerning sexuality are closely linked to issues of class. In the novel we can see how the group operates through a division of labour which characterises

the bourgeoisie. This is opposed to the older
aristocratic society which is typified by the Count.
The clashes in the novel therefore suggest a clash
between classes (although hardly a class war)
which is set-up as an historical clash between the
feudal and the modern. It is the Count who hordes
his money whereas the group use money as a
weapon, they bribe various officials and eye
witnesses and in so doing put money into
circulation, the proper place for it in the bourgeois
world. The Count is Other to the group on a
variety of levels. He is historically anachronistic,
he defies their ideas about what constitutes nature,
he is defined as inherently criminal, and he is
regarded as a sexual danger. What is significant in
this is the fashion in which these identities overlap
with each other, which means that the Count
functions on many different levels at the same
time.

Finally I looked at how writing is used in the novel
because this is not as straight forward as it might
appear. Rather we can see how writing is inflected
by the same types of issues which surround the
Count, writing indicates health, but it also suggests
the possibility of arriving at verifiable 'truths'. The
group function as nascent detectives as they hunt
through the narrative looking for clues. Writing
possesses problematics of its own, as I outlined
towards the end here, which can be tied to notions
of class and to ideas concerning sexuality.

Dracula is a complicated novel because of the
way in which it operates on many different levels
simultaneously, I have shown here how one issue

is inflected by another, and so on. The history of the criticism of the novel reflects the various complexities of the novel itself. In the following chapter I will outline some critical responses to **Dracula**; the critics which I discuss have made important contributions to placing the novel in certain contexts (psychoanalytical, historical, feminist), but, paradoxically are critics whose work is relatively difficult to find.

Chapter Three - The Critics

In this chapter I outline a series of readings of the
novel published in the late 1970's to the middle of
the 1980's. These interpretations of the novel have
all had some influence upon how the novel is
perceived and have therefore provided a critical
blueprint which is still followed by scholars today.
All of these articles have been published in a
variety of journals, and have been collated in one
volume, **The Vampire and The Critics** edited by
Margaret L. Carter (1). This volume is sadly out of
print and so this is an opportunity to resurrect
those readings which have provided critics with
important starting points. This is a very brief
account of these critics which I give here, but I
hope that readers will get some impression of the
direction which criticism on the novel has taken.
My reading of these critics cannot compensate for
looking at these articles in their own right but the
following arguments will help to highlight the
important developments made in the criticism of
Dracula.

Christopher Craft

In this section I will outline Christopher Craft's reading of **Dracula** '"Kiss Me with Those Red Lips": Gender and Inversion in Bram Stoker's **Dracula** (2), Craft uses a mixture of Freudian psychoanalysis and historical information in order to account for how Stoker's novel constructs an ambivalent portrait of gender.

Craft explores the historical moment which ratifies an unsettled relationship between gender distinctions. For Craft, **Dracula** evidences a concern that gender roles are fluid and this anxiety can be explained by an analysis of various philosophical and scientific texts of the time. Craft outlines John Addington Symonds book **A Problem in Modern Ethics** (1891) which explores issues of homosexual desire. Symonds established the idea that homosexuals were subject to a 'sexual inversion'. Such an inversion was associated with a natural state, 'sexual inverts' might have a marginal status but this should not detract from their essential sexuality. Symonds argument was an attempt to take sexuality out of the realm of moral debate and to place sexuality within a space which subjects it to a more rigorous scientific scrutiny. Craft writes that Symonds' work calls for the decriminalization of homosexuality by supplanting it with medicalization (p.174); effectively this meant replacing one form of policing with another. Homosexuality was conflated with the possession of feminine characteristics which were overly dominant in the male (the opposite being the case with lesbianism). Craft point out that this position excludes the notion that gender cannot be associated with sex designation, '[...]desire may not be gendered intrinsically as the body is, and that desire seeks its objects according to a complicated set of conventions that are culturally and institutionally determined' (p.174). The reason why such a position was obviated was because it suggested that all sexuality was socially ordained, as such heterosexuality would be understood as a socially given. The argument that some men possessed feminine souls is, for Craft, a suggestive one because it means that there is an implicit fashion in which masculine desire is 'feminized'. That is to say that desire, because it is associated with precise sex designation, is paradoxically unstable. Desire can take on a trajectory which is at odds with biology, such an argument really functions to expose the fact that gender is the key issue here (notwithstanding the attempts to deny this by people such as Symonds) so that by exploring how desire is structured along gender lines it means that we can explore a series of displacements between sex as something biologically given and gender as something culturally given. The way that this is exposed is because the notion of a feminine soul between attracted males reveals how homosexuality was accounted for in heterosexual terms. Craft writes that 'Desire between anatomical males requires the interposition of an invisible femininity, just as desire between anatomical females requires the mediation of a hidden masculinity' (p.175).

The connection between this type of information and **Dracula** is probably unclear at this stage, but

Craft proceeds to establish the idea that Stoker's novel evidences an anxiety about gender identity which reflects this problematic attempt to define authentic sexuality through these moments of heterosexual displacement.

Craft begins his analysis of these displacements through an analysis of the moments when distinctions break down. It is these moments which, for Craft, represent the collapse of gender identities which are to be found in the works of theorists such as Symonds. Crucially these moments are associated with the character of the vampire. He writes that Dracula '[...]is **nosferatu**, neither dead nor alive but somehow both, mobile frequenter of the grave and boudoir, easeful communicant of exclusive realms' (p.177). Scientists such as Dr Seward and Van Helsing are the celebrants and protectors of the very distinctions which the vampire threatens to erode. The battle between the Count and Van Helsing is one which takes place through women, a position which thus replicates the debate over the feminine intervention taking place between homosexuals; and which thus implies that the novel is reliant upon a submerged homoerotic impulse. Craft writes that 'This interposition of a woman between Dracula and Van Helsing should not surprise us; in England, as in Castle Dracula, a violent wrestle between males is mediated through a feminine form' (p.178). This idea that men only encounter each other through women is further reinforced by the blood transfusions undergone by Lucy. In effect the men put the blood into Lucy which the Count then takes out. Craft reads this as a symbolic passing on of semen. This is gestured to in the transfusions when Van Helsing characterises the procedure as constructing a kind of marriage between Lucy and the group. It is here that the men are connected to each other through a mingling of their blood/semen. The men meet each other through Lucy and then meet the Count through the blood that he removes.

It is this process of displacement which Craft also observes as taking place in the staking of Lucy, for him 'Lucy receives the phallic correction that Dracula deserves' (p.184). This means that what characterises the novel is a complicated series of transferences and displacements which were culturally sanctioned in scientific texts of the time. Issues surrounding homosexuality are always positioned at one remove from the male because of the function of a 'feminine' gender. This gender is merely a disguise which enables men to meet through feminine forms (such as the prone Lucy). This process is also at work in Mina's infection by the Count. For Craft, the scene where Mina drinks from a wound in the Count's chest represents another form of displacement which is revealed through the double nature of the symbolism of this moment. Following C.F. Bentley, Craft sees this scene as representing both an 'enforced fellation'(3) and a type of nursing. Mina is suckling the Count's breast in ways which echo the child - parent relationship. In this way the Count symbolises the mother, nurturing Mina by introducing her to the world of the vampire, but also Mina is forced to drink his blood which '"began to spurt"' and with her head held close to this wound '"I must either suffocate or swallow some of the - Oh, my God, my God! What have I done?"' (4); which also implies that once again, blood is associated with semen. Craft writes of this scene that the '[...]anatomical displacements and the confluence of blood, milk, and semen forcefully erase the demarcation separating the masculine and feminine' (p.186).

Craft's argument is therefore an attempt to locate **Dracula** within contemporary debates of the time. This is a useful way in which to contextualise the novel and it offers an alternative account of the novel's displacements. However, Craft does go on to discuss the novel in psychoanalytical terms which moves his reading away from a materialist critique to one more fully defined as Freudian. This reading appears in his account of the relationship between Id, Ego, and Superego. Craft quotes Freud from **The Ego and the Id** where he writes that:-

> From the point of view of instinctual control, of morality, it may be said of the id that it is totally non-moral, of the ego that it strives to be moral, and of the super-ego that it can be supermoral and then become as cruel as only the id can be (5).

This means that under certain circumstances the superego and the id cannot be properly separated. Craft's argument is that in the novel the Count consistently appears as the rebellious id who is opposed by a censorious superego (the opposing group). However, the group also have a particular sadism of their own which is manifested in their violent (and sexualised) staking of Lucy, for example. In this way the group and the Count are reflections of each other. It is for this reason that Harker, early on in the novel, is unable to see the reflection of the Count in the mirror, all Harker sees is a reflection of himself. Craft writes that:-

> The meaning of this little visual allegory should be clear enough: Dracula need cast no reflection because his presence, already established in Harker's image, would be simply redundant; the monster, indeed, is no one "except myself." A dangerous sameness waits behind difference; tooth, stake, and hypodermic needle, it would seem, all share a point (p.188).

I discussed in the previous chapter the relationship between the Count and the group, and it is possible to see here how an alternative perspective comes to similar conclusions in a rather different way. This conflation of the id with the superego is an argument which runs alongside Craft's other argument concerning the novel's implicit homosexuality. Craft, for example, reads the final scene of the novel, the image of the child who is named after the group, as representing the child as a 'son of an illicit and nearly invisible homosexual union' (p.189). This type of argument, despite its predominately avowed materialism, is inevitably ghosted by notions of the unconscious, because it is there that desire can be more substantively accounted for. Craft implicitly acknowledges this when he writes that, 'Men touching women touch each other, and desire discovers itself to be more fluid than the Crew of Light would consciously allow' (p.189). It is just such a reading which I will look at next.

Gail B. Griffin

Gail B. Griffin's article '"Your Girls That You All Love Are 'Mine'": **Dracula** and the Victorian Male Sexual Imagination.' (6) is a reading of the novel which identifies some of the novels more or less overtly misogynistic features. In particular Griffin argues that the novel evidences a masculine fear of the sexually empowered women. For this reason the female vampire is singled out as a specific source of revulsion. The notion of desire is important in this because it suggests a necessary ambivalence which defines the female vampire; she is both an object of desire and sexually debased. Griffin establishes this argument through the now commonplace assumption of the Victorian women as categorised as either 'angel' or 'whore'. Griffin does however take this a step further by suggesting that this is not a simple dichotomy, rather these two descriptions are interdependent. This is because the idealisation of women such as Lucy inevitably leads to, for Griffin, the transformation of the women into her opposite. The identification of the pre-vampiric Lucy as angelic is itself part of a misogynistic way of seeing which implies the existence of its other misogynistic polarity. Lucy is therefore both 'angel' and 'whore' simultaneously and this is evident in both the longing for her expressed by Arthur in the scene at the tomb, and the desire to destroy her. This points to a central ambivalence in the novel which is the male characters' urge to protect Lucy by destroying her in her vampire form.

Griffin points out that the Count is largely absent from the novel after the opening scenes. Sexuality, as something associated with desire does not play a part in the descriptions of the Count, instead it is initially the three female vampires at the castle who are eroticised. It is these three vampires who offer a direct threat to Harker, and this threat takes on the guise of a potential sexual assault. Griffin writes of Harker's erotic encounter with the vampires that 'For the first time vampirism is linked with stifled, obsessive sexuality, all the more urgent because forbidden;' (p.139). It is the female vampire who thus functions to awaken male desire whilst at the same time causing feelings of revulsion.

Griffin also spends some time exploring the scene where Lucy is staked in her tomb. For her, this scene implies that what is truly horrific is the sexualised woman. She points out that these scenes are highly sexually charged whereas the killing of the Count is understated. Other critics, such as Craft, have followed a Freudian line in identifying blood with semen. Such a reading takes into account the male's loss of blood but not the female's and this is something which Griffin attempts to readdress. She writes that 'The shedding of female blood is traditionally associated with two events in a woman's life: the loss of virginity and the menarche, both involving sexuality and concepts of defilement, impurity' (pp.141-2). For Griffin this can most clearly be observed in the descriptions of Mina after her force feeding of blood by the Count, here Mina in her despoiled gown and her protestation that she is '"unclean"' represents a menstruating woman who is 'unfit to touch a good man' (p.146). If Lucy is an object of revulsion because of her dangerous sexuality, then Mina is associated with menstrual impurity, and this is indicated by the maternal position which she occupies in the novel. Menstruation is therefore connected in the novel to notions of birth and so of motherhood.

It is when Mina has been 'cured' that her maternalism becomes fully in play, signalled in the final scene with her and her child. She is no longer an impure menstruating women. This is not to say that the novel easily separates the sexual women from the menstruating women. For Griffin, it is revealing that the female vampires are most frequently seen in the moonlight. She writes about this and menstruation that, 'The prominence of the moon and moonlight in the scene of female vampirism seems to support this connection, as the moon probably grew into a symbol for woman from its relation to the menstrual cycle' (p.142). In the Victorian period there existed a pseudo-scientific belief that the moon would induce personality changes (lunar and lunacy), and Griffin argues that Lucy is representative of this, 'Lucy is a horrible caricature of the "moody woman," ruled by the inconstant moon, victim of her own biology and subject to sudden, violent personality changes' (p.142). This means that in the novel women are closely associated with biological functions whereas the men are not. The reason for this, argues Griffin, is because of a wider malaise which is inherent to Victorian culture, she writes:-

> For the Victorian mind the threat of the beast within was particularly great, because of the immense tension surrounding sexuality, because of a larger fear of the irrational and the instinctual, and because Darwin had sensitized the whole of society to the proximity of simian ancestors (p.142).

Griffin acknowledges that the Count is also described in terms of animality (his metamorphoses into a bat or wolf), but sees this idea of the 'beast within' as being a central description of the dangers of the sexually active woman. Also, the danger of the sexually active women is that she contravenes the 'rule' of the maternal women, and this is something which is made clear in the descriptions of Lucy in her guise as the Bloofar Lady. Griffin writes about the discovery of Lucy with a child that:-

> When Lucy dashes her small victim to the ground, Stoker's point is clear: Dracula has so completely polluted her femininity that she has lost all maternal feeling. God's designated protector of children has become their predator. The transformation from woman to monster is complete (p.143).

Griffin's argument is an important one because it is essentially an exploration of the labelling of 'evil' in the novel. The sexually active women is the paradox in this, she is an object of desire and a 'monster' who undermines the pure, maternal woman. The category of 'angel' only masks this sexuality and in Dracula, for Griffin, '[...]the worst horror it can imagine is not Dracula at all but the released, transforming sexuality of the Good Woman' (p.148). Perhaps one feature which is not addressed by Griffin is the role that a construction of masculine desire plays in all of this. What is overlooked is that the women in the novel are also versions of certain male fantasies. This is clear in the scene of Harker's erotic encounter with the three female vampires. The novel certainly expresses a fear of the sexually active woman but it also sees such woman, at some level, as legitimate objects of desire. The failure to acknowledge this means that Griffin's argument is dangerously close to corroborating the novel's versions of female sexuality as something dangerously authentic which needs to be challenged. Griffin analyses an important subtext in all of this but it is not the full story. One way to investigate this further is to place the novel within a literary history which helps to locate the vampire in a literary tradition of 'rakes'. This is something which I look at in the next section.

Carol L. Fry and Judith Weissman

The two articles which I discuss here are one written by Carol L. Fry and one by Judith Weissman. Both of these articles are somewhat crude in their understanding of the Gothic, and this is largely because of the way that they tend to chart alternative literary traditions to the Gothic. These traditions are significant because it shows how **Dracula** draws upon certain devices which are familiar to non-Gothic writings. Although both

Fry and Weissman do not construct complex arguments, their work is of importance because it helps to provide an alternative context in which to place Stoker's novel. I will discuss Fry first.

Fry in 'Fictional Conventions and Sexuality in **Dracula**.' (7) places Stoker's novel in a tradition of writing which embraces writers as diverse as Richardson and Hardy. She sees eighteenth century fiction as being partially characterised by constructions of the 'rake' who seduces innocent and pure women. To this degree there exist similarities to this type of fiction and the way that the Count prays upon the pure in **Dracula**. She sees this tradition as being recast through the Gothic in the eighteenth and nineteenth centuries and draws parallels between the Count and the portraits of Gothic villains which can be found in the work of Radcliffe, Lewis, and Charles Maturin. These parallels are crude ones, being based upon physiognomical similarities between the villains, but it does show how Stoker is building upon already existing literary patterns in his novel. Her argument is that in the novel Stoker used '[...]melodramatic effects achieved through the manipulation of conventional characters' (p.38).

Fry does not go into any great depth in her article, meaning that writers are referred to but their novels are not systematically explored. This does however give the critic a broad outline in which to place the novel. She mentions Richardson for example, and an analysis of **Pamela** would reveal that there does exist a certain amount of description and content which echoes with

Dracula. Richardson's Pamela is characterised by a purity which enables her to resist the assaults made by Lord B. This purity is not just a physical one but is also spiritual. It is her possession of an ennobling puritanism which implies that there is a providential design which protects her (a theme returned to by Radcliffe). Lord B posses the characteristics of the rake, a rake who is eventually won over by this purity. This might appear to have a largely structural similarity to the way that the Count prays upon the innocent in **Dracula**, but this issue of religion is an important one and it is something which Weissman identifies in the novel as a pivotal paradox.

Weissman in 'Women and Vampires; **Dracula** as a Victorian Novel' (8) writes about Mina's appeal to the group that they should pity rather than revile the Count that:-

> As the virgin Mary intercedes with God for sinners, Mina uses her womanly power of pity to intercede with men even for the worst of criminals, insisting that even he can be redeemed. Her idea of dying to one's worse self so that the better self may live is the traditional Christian idea of dying to the flesh that the spirit may live: vampirism is only an extreme version of the evil of the body against which Christians have been told to fight for almost two thousand years. And Mina is the ideal Christian woman, recalling men to an ideal of charity and love through her holy influence (p.74).

The similarity between this and **Pamela** is clear, which in turn implies that what is central to the Gothic is its reliance upon notions of romance.

Radcliffe's novels, for example, are Gothic romances, typically being characterised by a tabooed love which is overcome (which is also true of Richardson's novel). In **Dracula** this also takes place through the idea that the Count releases the power of sexual desire which pollutes the flesh. In this way the Count can be seen as a part of lengthy genealogy of literary rakes. Weissman writes that, 'The sexually straightforward woman, a stock figure in much of English literature, virtually disappears from the novel after Fielding and Richardson - until she is resurrected by Bram Stoker in **Dracula** as a vampire' (p.69). Here Weissman puts the focus upon the sexually active woman and charts a literary trajectory which includes Chaucer's Criseyde, moves through Shakespeare (Cleopatra) and culminates with the eighteenth century picaresque novel. For Weissman the sexually active female is given its fairest representation in Fielding (a contentious point). According to this argument, every 'pure' woman suggests the existence of a predatory rake. Weissman sees this as typified in the novels of Richardson, her example is that of **Clarissa**; for her, Lovelace is the clearest origin for the literary rake.

Weissman's emphasis is upon the representation of women rather than the rake, and she proceeds to explore **Jane Eyre**. The infamous description of Bertha as a vampire bears some similarity to the sense of revulsion which is provoked by the three female vampires in Stoker's novel. For Rochester and Jane, Bertha is defined by a disabling animality, and the novel implies that Bertha is subject to excessive sexual cravings. As in **Dracula**, the flesh becomes polluted by desire, so that Bertha functions as a contrast with the more moderate inclinations of Jane. Weissman writes that, 'The vampire is only mentioned in **Jane Eyre**, but Charlotte Brontë clearly understands the psychological connection between sexuality and demonic blood-sucking. Neither the vampire nor the extremely sexual woman is important in the Victorian novel again until **Dracula**' (p.72).

Weissman and Fry's contextualisation of the novel is largely descriptive than analytical. However, neither takes their argument too far away from the identification of comparisons. It is helpful to see Stoker's novel as a part of an ongoing literary tradition but what also needs to be explored is the way that it reconstructs certain elements from that tradition in order to create its own version of events. **Dracula** does construct versions of both the rake and the sexually active woman and this suggests that it combines elements from both Fielding and Richardson rather than follows one or the other. The christian element plays an important role in the novel but this is associated with the pseudo-scientific puritanism of the opposing bourgeois group, it is not something inherent to 'innocent' women (as it is with Richardson). This means that there exist many important differences as well as similarities between Stoker's novel and the tradition from which it emerges. The location of **Dracula** within a wider Victorian literary culture also requires some consideration and this is something which is addressed by Mark M. Hennelly, jr which is the final article that I discuss below.

Hennelly

Hennelly in 'Dracula: The Gnostic Quest and Victorian Wasteland.' (9) sees **Dracula** as symptomatic of an anxious Victorian mentality. The novel dramatises an anxious duality which is present in other, non-Gothic, types of Victorian writing. For Hennelly, this is manifested in the doubt which is cast upon knowledge in the Victorian period. Old certainties such as those represented by religious faith are undermined by the emergence of scientific thought (Biology, Psychology, and so on), which creates a sense of epistemological crisis. This means that two metaphors dominate Victorian writing and these are, for Hennelly, the wasteland and the quest for knowledge. Hennelly charts such an anxiety through a literary genealogy which includes Tennyson's 'Morte d'Arthur', Browning's 'Childe Roland', Matthew Arnold's 'Dover Beach' and Dickens' representation of Coketown in **Hard Times**. What is shown in these representations is a fear that Victorian culture and society is developing a wasteland of its own; progress becomes thwarted because of an intellectual sterility which is symptomatic of a wider confusion concerning the state of certifiable knowledge. There is thus an anxiety that knowledge of the world is undermined by how that world 'feels' to live in. This is a complex point, but it signals that the Victorian temper is defined by a duality between epistemology and ontology. This is represented in **Dracula** through the way that beneath a faith in science there also exists a faith in the veracity of superstition (the lore of the vampire) and an anxious denial of what an 'authentic' sexuality may feel like.

Hennelly's argument is that this duality is indicated through the reflections which exist between life in London and life in Transylvania. Earlier, I discussed Christopher Craft's argument about the relationship between the group and the Count and Hennelly's reading heads in the same direction. Hennelly is, however, more concerned with the way that the two culture's in **Dracula**, London and Translyvania, represent complimentary visions of a wasteland which runs throughout Victorian literary culture in general. Hennelly's initial claim is that:-

> Dracula is an allegory of rival epistemologies in quest of a gnosis which will rehabilitate the Victorian wasteland; and as its conclusion dramatizes, this rehabilitation demands a **transfusion**, the metaphor is inevitable, from the blood-knowledge of Dracula. Caught between two worlds, the now anaemic nineteenth century all but dead, the twentieth powerless to be born without fertile, ideological conception, fin-de-siecle England desperately needs redemption (p.80).

The model of the gnostic quest is central to Hennelly's argument and signals that ultimate knowledge can result in a much needed sense of redemption. For Hennelly, the land of the Count and the more modern world of London share certain characteristics. He discusses Seward's sense of desolation when he looks out of a window in his asylum at the surrounding London area and contrasts it with Seward's feelings of despair, I quote the passage in full in Hennelly:-

> It was a shock to me to turn from the wonderful smoky beauty of a sunset over London, with its lurid lights and inky shadows and all the marvellous tints that come on foul clouds even as on foul water, and to realize all the grim sternness of my own cold stone building, with its wealth of breathing misery, and my own desolate heart to endure it all (pp.127-8, Hennelly p.80).

Within London then there is a pervasive sense of desolation, and this is not solely confined to Seward's mental state but, for Hennelly, is suggested throughout the novel. However, these moments are relatively discrete ones because the greatest site of desolation is associated with Transylvania. For Hennelly, this suggests that the opposing group map on their own sense of despair onto Translyvania, and the paradox is that a knowledge of its laws and customs will have a redemptive effect on their own wasteland. Inevitably it is the Count who is pivotal in this, because knowledge of him and his lore will provide a sense of salvation. Hennelly quotes at length the speech which Van Helsing makes about the Count and his past, I quote it here in full because it is central to his overall argument;

> I have told them how the measure of his leaving of his own barren land - barren of peoples - and coming to a new land where life of man teems till they are like the multitude of standing corn, was the

work of centuries. Were another of the Un-Dead, like him, to try to do what he has done, perhaps not all the centuries of the world that have been, or that will be, could aid him. With this one, all the forces of nature that are occult and deep and strong must have worked together in some wondrous way. The very place, where he have been alive, Un-Dead for all these centuries, is full of strangeness of the geologic and chemical world. There are deep caverns and fissures that reach none know whither. There have been volcanoes, some of whose openings still send out waters of strange properties, and gases that kill or make to vivify. Doubtless, there is something magnetic or electric in some of these combinations or occult forces which work for physical life in strange way; and in himself were from the first some great qualities. In a hard and warlike time he was celebrate that he have more iron nerve, more subtle brain, more braver heart, than any man. In him some vital principle have in strange way found their utmost; and as his body keep strong and grow and thrive, so his brain grow too. All this without that diabolic aid which is surely to him; for it to have to yield to the powers that come from, and are, symbolically of good (p.353, Hennelly p.81).

The implication is that the Count needs the world of the West in order to develop, but the West also needs him because he possesses certain assets which the West needs to know in order to ensure its redemption. The Count was once 'symbolic of good' a goodness which has turned to something more malign; if this transformation can be properly understood then the opportunity of escaping from the wasteland to a new utopia becomes possible. The Count is therefore the key to all of this because his moral decline echoes the moral decline of the West, to understand him is thus to understand the nature of that decline. Hennelly quotes from Elliot Gose's **Imagination Indulged: The Irrational in the Nineteenth Century Novel** a passage which will resonate with readers of **Dracula** although this is not a novel which Gose refers to. Gose writes that;-

> Beneath the ordered society of his time each [novelist of the Irrational] saw an unordered chaos, a world disintegrating, a new order waiting to be established. Each saw a spectacle, perhaps because it was true of Victorian society, but more fundamentally because each had descended within himself and confronted in that heart of darkness not only the death of life but the unborn shape of future life. Their novels embody that life (10).

What Hennelly identifies in **Dracula** is an attempt to 'redeem this wasteland' (p.82), and the way to achieve this is through a quest for an absolute knowledge. It is Transylvania which possesses this knowledge because it is through a knowledge of its superstitions that the Count can be overcome. In this argument the Count again dramatises something which is inherent to the group so that he loses his status of Other and becomes the receptacle of a troubling self-knowledge.

Hennelly points out that the novel constructs a series of competing knowledge claims, so that the novel works through the respective merits of Transcendentalism, Empiricism and the Philosophy of Crime, Superstition, and Scientific Rationalism. It is the claims of the latter which are subject to the deepest scrutiny, it is Van Helsing who demands that Dr Seward keeps an open mind concerning the superstitious faith in the existence of vampires. This means, for Hennelly, that **Dracula** is essentially celebrating the benefits of keeping an open mind which the faith in the claims of particular disciplines undermines, in this way the novel is highly sceptical about the state and status of Victorian knowledge. Hennelly also sees this as being signalled by the novel's epistolary form where each of the members are able to make their own contribution to the solving of the problem. In this way 'truth' becomes something which is open to discussion and revision, also '[...]the epistolary style always insists upon the relativity of knowledge and the problem of certainty' (p.83), its very multi-vocalism suggests that a monolithic sense of knowledge does not apply. The Count does not just gain knowledge but they also gain knowledge of him which is suggestive of an epistemological convergence. Hennelly also writes about the structure of the novel that:-

> In another sense, the disappearance of an omniscient narrator in Dracula reflects the atrophy of God and traditional faith so symptomatic of the Victorian wasteland: hence the small, central group of splintered selves is also searching for a new stockpile of communal and personal values (p.83).

It is perhaps for this reason that Van Helsing's quasi-Catholicism fails to protect lucy.

Hennelly also explores the similarities between the

Count's castle and Dr Seward asylum. These similarities support his argument that there exists an 'intimate identity between Transylvania and London' (p.84) in the novel. Hennelly writes that:-

> Dracula's castle is a schizoid dwelling with upper, fashionable apartments and even a Victorian library but also with lower crypts and vaults while, analogously, Dr Seward's Victorian mansion conceals a lunatic asylum, complete with fledgling vampire, beneath it (p.84).

Hennelly goes on to point out other echoes, 'Dracula was three lovers; Lucy has three suitors. Dracula hypnotizes; Van Helsing Hypnotizes. Dracula sucks blood; Van Helsing transfuses blood' (p.84). In this way the two countries are mirror-images of each other because they are essentially the same, a knowledge of Transylvania is a knowledge of London which will eradicate the sense of despair felt earlier by Dr Seward.

For this wasteland to be redeemed it also requires that the values of the old order should be overturned, and this old order is associated as much with Lord Godalming as it is with the Count. It is Arthur who appears to have an anomalous status in the opposing group because he is not one of the professional classes, rather he is representative of an aristocratic class which, in the guise of the Count is already in decline. Hennelly writes that 'Arthur Holmwood, or *Lord* Godalming, emblemizes class, wealth, and aristocratic values, all instances of decay in the Victorian wasteland' (p.85). Hennelly quotes

Northrop Frye on the status of the gentleman in the nineteenth century:-

> The ascendent class[...]and more particularly the aristocracy, comes to represent an ideal authority, expressed in the term 'gentleman,' at the point in history at which its effective temporal authority had begun to decline...The special function of the aristocracy has always included the art of putting on a show, of dramatizɪ ɪg a way of life (11).

Hennelly plays down Arthur's importance in the novel (ultimately he has no expertise, but is able to bankroll the adventure), '[...]Arthur's way of life is finally ineffectual; his aristocratic code is too divorced from natural values as symbolized by his replacement of the natural *Holmwood* with the divine-right (*God-*) of noblesse oblige pedigree (*-alming*)' (p.86).

So then, according to Hennelly the novel charts the decline of the aristocracy and the emergence of a new bourgeois class whose expertise supplants them. This emergence is tinged with its own anxieties because this expertise is thrown into doubt. What **Dracula** does is stage a debate between various new epistemologies before it looks back to a form of vampire lore which is to be found in superstitious belief. This return to the past is ultimately given a scientific credence by Van Helsing who is able to map on contemporary criminology (Lombroso and Nordau) in order to explain the irredeemability of the Count. It is this irredeemability which supplies the back-drop against which the Victorian wasteland can be redeemed. The bourgeois group discover a new kind of knowledge which is a composite of many forms (science, criminology, superstition) which implies the possibility of a totalising knowledge. At the close of the novel this all appears to be thrown in doubt with the reader's credence being appealed to. However, it is the child, for Hennelly, which signifies that a new order has been confirmed and which suggests the possibility of progress. Hennelly writes of this final scene that:-

> Finally, we hear that "There have been from the loins of this very one [Dracula] great men and good women" (p.265); and this anticipates the birth of the Harker child through whose veins run not only the Victorian blood of his parents but also the vitality of the Count whose blood Mina has drunk. And this new, twentieth-century Fisher King, appropriately born on the anniversary of Dracula's death, not only represents the ancient blood-knowledge of his second father; but shoring these fragments against England's ruin, "his bundle of names links all" the allegorical epistemologies of the "little band of men together" (p.218).

The strength of Hennelley's reading is that it enables the novel to be located within a wider Victorian culture which is not simply identified by structural similarities (as Fry and Weissman do). It is also a reading of the novel which historicises the novel's dualities rather than mapping them through an ahistorical account of Freudian categories. It also helps to explain why the novel sets up an opposition between East and West which, on closer examination, becomes elided through a process of epistemological reflection.

In this chapter I have outlined a series of readings of the novel which are difficult to obtain. The interest in **Dracula** has to some degree moved on from these readings but more recent criticism is indebted to them because their arguments still bear relevance. In the bibliography I give a list of sources which readers will find provide helpful frames in which to discuss the novel.

Chapter One - The Gothic

Notes

1. Edmund Burke, **A Philosophical Enquiry into the Origins of our Ideas of The Sublime and The Beautiful,** (1757) Trans James T. Boulton, (Oxford, 1987).

2. Immanuel Kant, 'Analytic of the Sublime' in **The Critique of Judgement,** Part One, (1790) Trans James Creed Meredith, (Oxford, 1986) pp.90-203.

3. Ann Radcliffe, **The Mysteries of Udolpho,** (1794) (Oxford, 1988).

4. Ellen Moers, **Literary Women,** (London, 1978).

5. Matthew Lewis, **The Monk,** (1796) (Oxford, 1987).

6. David Punter, **The Literature of Terror: A History of Gothic Fictions from 1765 to the Present Day,** (London, 1989).

7. Ann Radcliffe, **The Italian,** (1797) (Oxford, 1987).

8. Mary Shelley, **Frankenstein: or the Modern Prometheus,** (1831) (Harmondsworth, 1985).

9. Chris Baldick, **In Frankenstein's Shadow: Myth, Monstrosity, and Nineteenth-Century Writing,** (Oxford, 1990).

10. My argument here follows that of David Punter's in **The Literature of Terror**.

11. Mary Poovey, **The Proper Lady and the Woman Writer: Ideology as Style in the Works of Mary Wollstonecraft, Mary Shelley, and Jane Austen**, (London, 1984) p.126.

12. Rosemary Jackson, **Fantasy: The Literature of Subversion**, (London, 1986).

Chapter Two - Sex and Text; The Problem of 'Truth' in Dracula.

1. Bram Stoker, **Dracula**, (1897) (Harmondsworth, 1979).

2. Michel Foucault, **The History of Sexuality** (vol 1) Trans Robert Hurley (Harmondsworth, 1990).

3. Francis Barker, **The Tremulous Private Body**, (London, 1984).

4. See Rosemary Jackson's **Fantasy** for her Lacanian reading of this moment pp.120-1.

⳾ 5. Leonard Woolf, **Annotated Dracula**, (London, 1975) p.300.

6. Carol A. Senf, '**Dracula**: The Unseen Face in the Mirror' in **The Vampire and the Critics**,
   ⳾ ed Margaret L. Carter, (London, 1988) p.101.

Chapter Three - The Critics.

1. Margaret L. Carter, **The Vampire and the** ×
   Critics, (London, 1988).

2. Christopher Craft, '"Kiss me with those red
   lips": Gender and Inversion in Bram Stoker's
   Dracula' in Carter pp.167-194.

3. C.F. Bentley, 'The Monster in the Bedroom,
   Sexual Symbolism in Bram Stoker's **Dracula**'
   in **Literature and Psychology**, 22 (1972) p.30
   cited in Craft p.185.

4. p.343 in **Dracula** cited in Craft p.185.

5. Sigmund Freud, **The Ego and the Id** (New
   York, 1960) pp.44-45 cited in Craft p.187.

6. Gail B. Griffin, '"Your Girls That You All
   Love Are Mine": **Dracula** and the Victorian
   Male Sexual Imagination' in Carter pp.137-
   148.

7. Carol L. Fry, 'Fictional Conventions and
   Sexuality in **Dracula**' in Carter pp.35-38.

8. Judith Weissman, 'Women and Vampires:
   Dracula as a Victorian Novel' in Carter
   pp.69-77.

9. Mark M. Hennelly Jr, '**Dracula**: The Gnostic
   Quest and the Victorian Wasteland' in Carter
   pp.79-92.

10. Elliot Gose, **Imagination Indulged: The Irrational in the Nineteenth Century Novel,** (Montreal, 1972) p.176 cited in Hennelly p.82.

11. Northrop Frye, **Backgrounds to Victorian Literature**, ed Richard Levine, (San Francisco, 1967) p.126 cited in Hennelly p.86.

Arata, Stephen D. (1990), 'The Occidental Tourist: Dracula and the Anxiety of Reverse Colonisation', **Victorian Studies**, 33: 621-45.

Astle, Richard (1980), 'Dracula as Totemic Monster: Lacan, Freud, Oedipus and History', **Sub-stance**, 25: 98-105.

Bentley, C.F. (1972), 'The Monster in the Bedroom, Sexual Symbolism in Bram Stoker's Dracula', **Literature and Psychology**, 22. Also in Carter.

Brantlinger, Patrick (1988), **Rule of Darkness: British Literature and Imperialism, 1830-1914**, New York.

Byers, Thomas B. (1988), 'Good Men and Monsters: The Defenses of Dracula', in Carter.

Case, Sue-Ellen (1991), 'Tracking the Vampire', **Differences**, 3: 1-20.

Carter, Margaret L. (ed), (1988), **The Vampire and the Critics**, London.

Copjec, Joan (1991), 'Vampires, Breast-Feeding, and Anxiety', **October**, 58: 25-43.

Craft, Christopher (1988), '"Kiss me with those red lips": Gender and Inversion in Bram Stoker's **Dracula**' in Carter.

Select Bibliography - Dracula and Related Criticism

95

Cranny-Francis, Anne (1988), 'Sexual Politics and Political Repression in Bram Stoker's Dracula', in Clive Bloom et al (eds), **Nineteenth Century Suspense: From Poe to Conan Doyle**, Basingstoke.

Dijkstra, Bram (1986), **Idols of Perversity: Fantasies of Feminine Evil in Fin-de-Siecle Culture**, Oxford.

Dingley, R.J. (1991), 'Count Dracula and the Martians' in Kath Filmer (ed) **The Victorian Fantasists**, Basingstoke.

Dukes, Paul (1982), 'Dracula: Fact, Legend, Fiction', **History Today**, 32.

Dyer, Richard (1988), 'Children of the Night: Vampirism as Homosexuality, Homosexuality as Vampirism', in Susannah Radstone (ed) **Sweet Dreams: Sexuality, Gender and Popular Fiction**, London.

Dyer, Richard (1993), 'Dracula and Desire', **Sight and Sound**, 3: 8-12.

Fontana, Ernest (1988), 'Lombroso's Criminal Man and Stoker's Dracula' in Carter.

Frayling, Christopher (ed) (1991), **Vampyres**, London.Fry, Carol L. (1988), 'Fictional Conventions and Sexuality in **Dracula**', in Carter.

Frost, Brian J. (1989), **The Monster with a Thousand Faces: Guises of the Vampire in Myth and Literature**, Ohio.

Gelder, Ken (1994), **Reading the Vampire**, London.

Griffin, Gail B. (1988), '"Your Girls That You All Love are Mine": **Dracula** and the Victorian Male Sexual Imagination' in Carter.

Hatlen, Burton (1988), 'The Return of the Repressed/Oppressed in Bram Stoker's **Dracula**', in Carter (1988).

Hennelly, Mark M. Jr. (1988), **'Dracula: The Gnostic Quest and Victorian Wasteland'** in Carter.

Jackson, Rosemary (1981), **Fantasy: The Literature of Subversion**, London. Johnson, Alan. P. (1984), '"Dual Life": The Status of Women in Stoker's Dracula', **Sexuality and Victorian Literature**, 20-39.

Jones, Ernest (1991), 'On the Vampire', in Christopher Frayling (ed), **Vampyres**, London.

Kirtley, Bacil F. (1988) ' Dracula, the Monastic Chronicles and Slavic Folklore' in Carter.

Kittler, Friedrich (1989), 'Dracula's Legacy', **Stanford Humanities Review**, 1: 143-173.

Leatherdale, Clive (1985), **Dracula: The Novel and the Legend**, Northamptonshire.

Martin, Philip (1988), 'The Vampire in the Looking-Glass: Reflection and Projection in Bram Stoker's **Dracula'** in Bloom et al

Moretti, Franco (1988), 'Dialectic of Fear', in **Signs Taken for Wonders: Essays in the Sociology of Literary Form**, London.

Pope, Rebecca A. (1990), 'Writing and Biting in **Dracula', Literature, Interpretation, Theory**, 1: 199-216.

Punter, David (1989), **The Literature of Terror: A History of Gothic Fictions from 1765 to the prsent Day**, London
Richardson, Maurice (1991), 'The Psychoanalysis of Count Dracula', in Frayling.
Roth, Phyllis A. (1988), 'Suddenly Sexual Women in Bram Stoker's **Dracula'** in Carter.

Senf, Carol A. (1988), 'Dracula: the Unseen Face in the Mirror' in Carter.

Skal, David J. (1990), **Hollywood Gothic: The Tangled Web of 'Dracula' from Novel to Stage to Screen**, New York.
Twitchell, James (1988), 'The Vampire Myth' in Carter.

Wall, Geoffrey (1984), '"Different from Writing": Dracula in 1897', **Literature and History**, 10: 15-23.

Weissman, Judith (1988), 'Women and Vampires: **Dracula** as a Victorian Novel' in Carter.

Wicke, Jennifer (1992), 'Vampiric Typewriting: **Dracula** and Its Media', **English Literary History**, 59: 467-493.

Woolf, Leonard (ed) (1975), **Annotated Dracula**, London.

Zanger, Jules (1991), 'A Sympathetic Vibration: **Dracula** and the Jews', **English Literature in Transition 1880-1920**, 34: 33-44.